Secrets of the
Sixth Edition

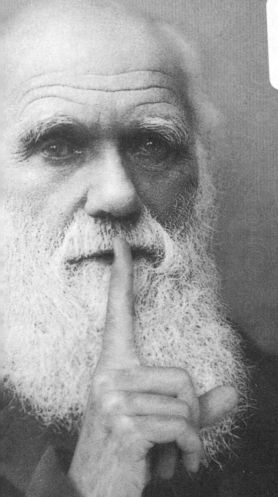

Master Books®
A Division of New Leaf Publishing Group
www.masterbooks.net

Secrets of the Sixth Edition

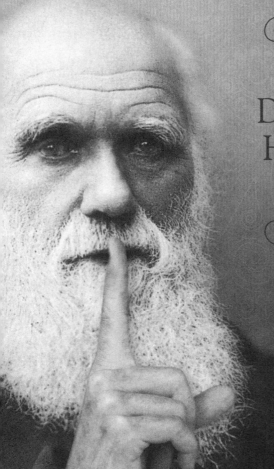

Darwin
Discredits
His Own
Theory

RANDALL HEDTKE

First printing: 1983
First Master Books printing: August 2010

ISBN: 978-0-89051-597-6
Library of Congress Number: 2010932845

Cover by Left Coast Design, Portland, Oregon

Please consider requesting that a copy of this volume be purchased by your local library system.

Printed in the United States of America

Please visit our website for other great titles:
www.masterbooks.net

For information regarding author interviews,
please contact the publicity department at (870) 438-5288.

Master
Books®
A Division of New Leaf Publishing Group
www.masterbooks.net

Contents

Evolution is purported to be a scientific theory; therefore, all teachers have an unassailable right to question the evidence in the classroom. Not only an exalted right but a common sense expectation, and an invulnerable obligation to students and the science.

— Randall Hedtke

Foreword

What is the secret of the sixth edition of *On the Origin of Species*? Incredibly, Charles Darwin, in his old age, abandoned natural selection, the mechanism by which evolution was believed possible. The reader may well ask how something of that significance could have remained a secret for so long when the sixth and last edition of the *Origin* was published in 1872. The primary reason why Darwin's secret had not previously been revealed to the public may simply be because few people bother to read the *Origin*. The book is probably one of the most-quoted or paraphrased, but least read books in the world. The *Origin* is seldom read for two reasons. First, Darwin's writing style was wordy, repetitious, and vague; consequently, few people have the mental stamina or desire to read the book from the beginning to the end. Second, there is little reason why anyone would want to read the *Origin*, since the basic concept of natural selection, or survival of the fittest, is explained in just a few sentences in most high school or college textbooks. I dare say that a survey of the general public or even of high school or university biology instructors would reveal a very low percentage who have actually read the sixth edition or any other edition of the *Origin*.

The larger question as to why Darwin abandoned natural selection, a hypothesis that is often placed on a par with Newtonian physics or Einstein's relativity, requires an intimate understanding of Darwin himself. It has been over ten years since I discovered, while studying the *Origin*, that Darwin had, inconceivably, abandoned his life's work. It was precisely because it was so inconceivable that Darwin would abandon natural selection that the knowledge languished in my mind and in my notebook for so long. I had, in the interim, occupied my spare time by researching and publishing other aspects of evolutionary views. It was not until reading two recently published books about Darwin's illness, which I had previously understood to be hypochondria but which is revealed in the books to be an anxiety-caused psychoneurosis, that I had reason for what had formerly seemed so unreasonable. The first investigation, *Secrets of the Sixth Edition*, provides evidence and the reasons why Darwin abandoned natural selection. The following investigations pertain to other closely related aspects of his hypothesis.

The last chapter, "The Principle of Applied Creation in an Origins Curriculum," describes the curriculum strategy that I developed and have taught for many years. The curriculum avoids the civil rights problem of separation of church and state. On the other hand, the curriculum does restore a basic human right formerly missing in the evolution curriculum, namely the right of every student to learn about alternative points of view or, as I described it in the essay, freedom of thought. On this point the code of ethics of the education profession adopted by the National Education Association is quite clear: "In fulfillment of the obligation to the student, the educator shall not unreasonably deny the student access to varying points of view." I am sure everyone in education would agree that is a commendable obligation to students. The concept of creation in the curriculum is used in a secular way to fulfill that obligation. Conversely, evolutionary theorists wish to have the scientific evidence for the origin of life interpreted exclusively from an evolutionary point of view. That being the case, the controversy is basically between the evolutionary theorist's scientific *modus operandi* and the education profession's code of ethics. My experience has taught me that freedom of thought prevails over any scientific *modus operandi*.

Finally, I hope the reader will excuse some repetition that was allowed to remain in the essays, taking into consideration that they were written over a period of 11 years and deal with overlapping subject matter.

Chapter 1

An Introduction to the Evolutionary Hypothesis

A Presentation of the Founders

It is only natural that in any drama, and the evolution controversy certainly is one, the principal players should be introduced at the outset. These consist of Charles Darwin, the author of the controversial view of the origin of life, and those who were in frequent and personal contact with him, his lieutenants, as one author called them.

Charles Darwin (1809–1882)

Charles was the son of Robert, a successful country physician whose father, Erasmus, grandfather to Charles, also had a successful medical practice. Erasmus had, during his lifetime, gained considerable recognition for his writings in the area of organic evolution, and it is his ideas that form the foundation for Charles's book *On the Origin of Species* published in 1859.

Charles attended Edinburgh and Cambridge without being attracted to any particular profession. He did not wish to follow in his father's and grandfather's footsteps as a physician, since for one thing, he had discovered that the dissecting of cadavers made him ill. At one time, he entertained the thought of entering the ministry and devoting his spare time to science, which is what he may have done had an uncle not arranged a position for him aboard the sailing ship *Beagle* on a government-sponsored exploration voyage. During the five-year voyage, Charles, the ship's naturalist, kept copious notes on his observations and collected and preserved numerous specimens. One of his first accomplishments shortly after his return to England was to publish a journal of the voyage and a description of the many specimens.

In 1839 Charles married a cousin, Emma Wedgewood. They resided in London for about two years and then bought a house near the village of Down about 15 miles from London. It was while living in London that Charles chose his life's occupation, which was to continue his grandfather's work on evolutionary ideas. Having an adequate inheritance, he retired to Down, and his life thereafter was characterized by a single-minded devotion to the cause of evolution, as this excerpt from his autobiography indicates:

> Few persons can have lived a more retired life than we have done. Besides short visits to the houses of the relations, and occasionally to the seaside or elsewhere, we have gone nowhere. During the first part of our residence we went a little into society, and received a few friends; but my health almost always suffered from the excitement, violent shivering and vomiting attacks being thus brought on. I have, therefore, been compelled for many years to give up all dinner parties; and this has been somewhat a deprivation to me, as such parties always put me into high spirits. From the same cause I have been able to invite here very few scientific acquaintances. My chief enjoyment and sole employment throughout life has been scientific work; and the excitement from such work makes me, for the time, forget, or drives right away my daily discomfort. I have, therefore, nothing to record during the rest of life except the publication of my several books.[1]

Nearly all of the publications to which he refers were written for the express purpose of enhancing the credibility of the hypothesis contained in the *Origin*. Although Charles enjoyed robust health during his youth and while aboard the *Beagle,* symptoms of a psychoneurosis began to appear shortly after his marriage. The illness continued throughout most of his life, with Emma becoming much like a nurse and mother, not only to Charles but to the ten children she raised.

Alfred R. Wallace (1823–1913)

A.R. Wallace was a self-made naturalist whose limited formal schooling was compensated by unlimited interest and enthusiasm. He traveled widely and endured numerous hardships in his zeal to collect specimens, which he studied and sold. Like so many others in his day, he too was preoccupied with the idea of discovering a materialistic explanation for the origin of life. In January 1858, on the small unexplored island of Ternate, while ill with a fever, the natural selection hypothesis suddenly occurred to him.

> One day something brought to my recollection Malthus's *Principle of Population*, which I had read about twelve years before. I thought of his clear exposition of "the positive checks to increase" — disease, accidents, war, and famine. . . . It then occurred to me that these causes or their equivalents are continually acting in the case of animals also. . . . Vaguely thinking over the enormous and constant destruction which this implied, it occurred to me to ask the question, "Why do some die and some live?" And the answer was clearly that on the whole the best fitted lived. . . . Then suddenly it flashed upon me that this self-acting process would necessarily *improve the race* because in every generation the inferior would inevitably be killed off and the superior would remain — that is, *the fittest would survive*.[2]

As soon as the fever left him, Wallace spent a few days developing the hypothesis in more detail and sent it off to Darwin. Much to his disappointment, Darwin read a hypothesis almost identical to the one he had been working on for some 20 years and at first assumed that priority for it would go to Wallace. Darwin's priority, though, was established by an 1844 sketch that he had written, and in 1859, about a year after receiving Wallace's paper, Darwin published the *Origin,* but A.R. Wallace's name had become inseparably linked to Darwin.

Sir Joseph Dalton Hooker (1817–1911)

Joseph Hooker was one of Darwin's oldest and perhaps closest friends, confiding in him as early as 1844 about his endeavor to formulate a credible hypothesis of evolution for the origin of life. Hooker's specialty was in the area of plant taxonomy, and during his career he contributed to scientific publications for many years. In 1865 he succeeded his father as director of Kew Gardens, a position that he held for many years. The other founders of evolutionary views were acquaintances of Darwin through a mutual interest in the view, but Hooker's relationship to Darwin seemed to have been one of genuine friendship.

Sir Charles Lyell (1797–1875)

Lyell was originally trained as a lawyer but found his true vocation as a geologist. He was both Darwin's mentor and his most frustratingly recalcitrant follower. In 1831 he published *Principles of Geology*, which had the distinction of establishing the concept of uniformitarian geology as opposed to what was then in vogue: catastrophic geology. According to uniformitarian geology, all of the geologic features of the earth's crust came into being by continuous processes presently operating. One can see, then, that the uplifting of a mountain range or the excavation of a Grand Canyon would take an exceedingly long time. Catastrophic geology, on the other hand, would postulate that mountain ranges were uplifted in the past by extraordinary forces not presently operating or that the Grand Canyon was excavated by a much greater volume of water before the sediment had solidified into sedimentary rock, consequently requiring a much shorter period of time.

Lyell's *Principles* was one of the books that Darwin had with him while aboard the *Beagle*. Evolutionary views and uniformitarian geology fit hand in glove; one enhances the credibility of the other. There can be no Darwinian evolution within the short time frame of catastrophic geology. Uniformitarian geology has the potential to push the age of the earth back to infinity, consequently creating a time frame long enough for Darwin's alleged organic evolution to take place.

Incredibly, Lyell was not an evolutionist. His thinking in regard to living things was not consistent with the continuous-processes thesis of uniformitarian geology. For the creation and extinction of living things, he called upon catastrophic or miraculous forces. Lyell's uniformitarian geology, with its extended time frame, cleared the way for evolutionary views, yet evolution was personally unacceptable to him. Perhaps for these reasons Darwin regarded Lyell as his barometer for success; if Lyell could be converted, then he could rest content. Darwin seemed to need the approval of Lyell in order to still his own doubts about his views. When Hooker suggested that Lyell was reacting favorably to the hypothesis, Darwin immediately wrote a letter of joy and relief to Lyell: "I rejoice profoundly; for, thinking of so many cases of men persuing an illusion for years . . . I have asked myself whether I may not have devoted my life to a phantasy."[3]

Darwin's joy was premature. Although he kept hinting that he would, Lyell never announced his conversion. Nevertheless, this did not prevent him from promoting Darwin's hypothesis. Since it enhanced his own geology views, he had a professional, vested interest for doing so.

Asa Gray (1810–1888)

Gray originally trained as a physician but found his niche as the leading American botanist at Harvard. If Lyell was recalcitrant, Gray was downright rebellious by comparison. Gray had been groomed by Darwin before the *Origin* was published to spread the word of his hypothesis in the United States. Gray faithfully performed this duty

He arranged for the publication of the *Origin,* defended it against criticism, and wrote favorable reviews. Like Huxley and Lyell, Gray performed the duties that Darwin desired, yet held serious reservations about the hypothesis.

In his book of essays on evolutionary views entitled *Darwiniana,* he consistently urged those who would reject it not to be hasty, and those who would accept it, not to do so prematurely. In regard to natural selection, Darwin's alleged mechanism for evolution, Gray states: "We believe that species vary and that 'natural selection' works; but we suspect that its operation, like every analogous natural operation, may be limited by something else."[4] In other words, he was denying Darwin's thesis that nature could select variations that would accumulate into new species.

Gray eventually had a falling-out with Darwin over the question of design. Gray could look around and see evidence of design in nature indicating to him the result of intelligence, not chance. Would Darwin base his views on theism or atheism? Darwin chose atheism, and with that decision Gray could no longer count himself among Darwin's inner circle of friends, although an apparently cordial relationship did continue.

Thomas Henry Huxley (1825–1895)

T.H. Huxley was in his day what we would today describe as an antiestablishment leader. He was an immensely popular fellow with an inexhaustible amount of energy and ambition that he directed not only against the religious establishment (he coined the word agnosticism) but against any social and educational inequities that came to his attention.

Were he alive today, he would certainly have become an ally in the feminist movement. He pioneered in the area of women's rights in higher education and against archaic laws that discriminated against them. He possessed a complete disregard for traditions or social mores that in his opinion favored the establishment at the expense of the masses. At one time his daughter Ethel wished to marry the widower of her deceased sister, Marion. There was a law in England at the time against marriages of this sort, and in protest to the law and in sympathy for his daughter, he took her to Norway where the marriage was consummated.

Something of Huxley's character is revealed in his personal letters, which frequently contained warlike similes directed against the opposition. Bibby describes the estimation others had of Huxley's ability and intellect.

> Wallace experienced in his presence a feeling of awe and inferiority which neither Darwin or Lyell produced; both Darwin and Hooker declared that in comparison with Huxley they felt quite infantile in intellect. And it was not a narrow or merely scholastic sort of intellect; it was many-dimensioned and as effective in practical affairs as in abstract reasoning. As a modern American writer has perhaps too colorfully put it, "Huxley had more talents than two lifetimes could have developed. He could think, draw, speak, write, inspire, lead, negotiate, and wage multifarious war against earth and heaven with the cool professional ease of an acrobat supporting nine people on his shoulders at once."[5]

All of this energy, ability, and intelligence was directed at making a name for himself. To his sister he wrote:

> I will leave my mark somewhere, and it shall be clear and distinct: T.H.H., his mark, and free from the abominable blur

of cant, humbug, and self-seeking which surrounds everything in this present world — that is to say, supposing that I am not already unconsciously tainted myself, a result of which I have a morbid dread.[6]

It is no wonder that the reclusive Darwin was overjoyed when Huxley found favor with his hypothesis and agreed to publicly defend it. It is no wonder, also, that Huxley should be attracted to evolutionary views as a weapon against established religion, which was anathema to him.

Huxley's scientific credentials were mainly in the area of comparative anatomy and taxonomy. He defended the hypothesis enthusiastically, albeit with some very important reservations that perhaps were not consistently and fairly expressed to his constituents.

It is ironic that the mark that Huxley achieved should be most popularly recognized as that of "Darwin's bulldog," a subordinate position to a man of lesser talents. Huxley is said to have enjoyed the luxuries of genius while Darwin possessed the bare essentials.

St. George Mivart (1827–1900)

St. George Mivart, an English biologist, was, like Lyell, educated for the bar but devoted himself to the biological sciences. Although an evolutionist of sorts, he was not a supporter of Darwin's natural selection mechanism. It was Mivart's criticisms to which Darwin responded in the sixth edition of the *Origin*. These criticisms forced concessions from Darwin that were tantamount to abandoning his natural selection mechanism, the warp and woof of evolutionary views.

The Social Darwinists

Last but by no means least, we cannot forget the social Darwinists, perhaps the most forceful of all the champions of the hypothesis. Their enthusiasm for evolutionary views were only surpassed by their ignorance about its finer points. These were the numerous writers of Darwin's day and after who possessed the mental capability to somehow make the connection that any kind of *change* — social, political, personality, or whatever — was evidence that organic change was possible. With their constant literary references to evolutionary views, they succeeded in making it a public fad while the question of its validity became passé. It was not the scientific accuracy of evolutionary theory that appealed to their minds, but the philosophy behind it that held them in rapture. Evolution scientists owe more than they admit to the social Darwinists and their "evolutionism."

Historical Background

No student of evolutionary views can claim to understand Darwin and the phenomenal acceptance of his hypothesis without taking into consideration the cultural times in which his book, *On the Origin of Species,* was published.

Well over 100 years ago, when the industrial or scientific revolution was new and in full swing, a handful of dedicated men were able to convince much of Western civilization that life had originated from some primordial soup in the oceans and continued to evolve into the great diversity of life that we see today, guided by little more than chance gene mutations acted upon by natural selection.

This was no small accomplishment and would have been doomed to failure like all of the previous attempts to formulate a materialistic explanation for origins had it not been for the opportune times in which the *Origin* was published. The success factor was not the invincible evidence or the soundness of the hypothesis, but the utopian dream of a new world wrought by science. This dream that nearly everyone shared placed the public in an ingenuous frame of mind. Were not evolutionary views delivered to us under the auspices of science? Are not scientists the great benefactors of our time? Is not the scientific method infallible? Seldom in the history of mankind had the power and prestige of a fraternal group risen so rapidly and to such dizzying heights as that of the scientific community. Macaulay, a noted British historian, exemplifies the public attitude of his time.

Macaulay was full of admiration for the scientific revolution he was witnessing in the early 19th century, and in this, as in so many things, he typified his age. For him as for others, then and now, "science" meant only partly empiricism, a method of looking at data. More immediately, more tangibly, "science" meant the secondary results of that method: the products of technology. During the long reign of Queen Victoria, "science" transformed many of the conditions of people's lives. The first railroad was built in England in 1825 when

Victoria was a little girl; before that, the maximum speed of land travel was, for up-to-date Englishmen as it had been for Caesars and Pharaohs, the speed of the horse. But before the queen and empress died, almost all of Britain's now existing railroads had been built; "science" had begun that liberation of man from animal muscle, that acceleration toward inconceivable velocities which is so characteristic of our own age and is still as impressive to us as it was to the Victorians.

Impressive: "science" was *doing* things, making things *work*. The practical, empirical, positivistic British temperament was fascinated. While Victoria occupied the throne, transatlantic steamship service was begun; power-driven machines revolutionized industry; the telegraph became a practical instrument and the telephone was developed; the electric lamp and the automobile were produced. Eight years before the *Origin*, the Victorians celebrated *Progress* at the first world's fair in the fabulous Crystal Palace where Macaulay felt as reverent as at St. Peter's. "Science" was making things happen; it could predict their occurrence; its success precluded doubt. It seemed to many at the time final and unambiguous. One could depend on it.[7]

Evolutionary views arose by science and by science it must stand or fall, and yet it soon happened that the hypothesis became instead a popular ethical, social, and philosophical concept that permeated nearly every aspect of Western culture.

Persuasive because "science" was persuasive, evolution became a watchword to the late Victorians. By the end of the century, hardly a field of thought remained unfertilized by the new concept. Historians had begun looking at the past as a "living organism"; legal theorists studied the law as a developing social institution; critics examined the evolution of literary types; anthropologists and sociologists invoked natural selection in their studies of social forms; apologists for the wealthy showed how the poor are the unfit and how progress under the leadership of the fit was inevitable; novelists "observed" their creatures as they evolved in an "empirical" way; and poets hymned a creative lifeforce.[8]

The social Darwinists had become an unexpected and powerful ally to the evolutionary movement. The social, ethical, and philosophical selling points propogated by the proponents of evolutionary views and enforced by the Victorians' overriding awe of science became the chief defenses for the evolutionary hypothesis. Indeed, the Victorians followed Darwin blindly. The evolutionist philosophers were soon on the offensive. Who would dare to question their interpretation of the evidence? Some theologians dared, but they were dismissed as religious bigots. After all, are not scientists paragons of objectivity? George Bernard Shaw candidly states:

> Never in history, as far as we know, had there been such a determined, richly subsidized, politically organized attempt to persuade the human race that all progress, all prosperity, all salvation, individual and social, depend on an unrestrained conflict for food and money, on the suppression and elimination of the weak by the strong, on free trade, free contract, free competition, natural liberty, laissez-faire: in short, on "doing the other fellow down" with impunity.[9]

Charles S. Pierce arrived at a similar conclusion that Darwin's hypothesis was nowhere near to be proved, but its favorable reception "was plainly owing, in large measure, to its ideas being those toward which the age was favorably disposed, especially, because of the encouragement it gave to the greed-philosophy."[10] The hypothesis had become, to a large degree, removed from accountability to the scientific community that had produced it.

Darwin's Obsession with His Book

Charles Darwin's writing career produced several books and papers in addition to his principal work, *On the Origin of Species,* which introduced his hypothesis of evolution. All of his other works, such as *The Descent of Man*, are subsidiaries to the *Origin*. Considering that he spent half of his entire lifetime writing and rewriting the *Origin*, the book was more than his major writing effort — it was his life's obsession. For example, he began earnestly taking notes in 1837, after his return from the exploration voyage aboard the *Beagle*, which put his age at 28. The first edition of the *Origin* was published in 1859 when he was 50, and the sixth and last revised edition was published in 1872 when he was 63. He died in 1882 at the age of 73. The actual span of time that he spent periodically writing and rewriting the *Origin* was approximately 36 years — half of his entire lifetime.

Many of the changes made in the *Origin* are what appear to be pointless word changes that do not improve the sentence structure nor change the meaning of a statement. On the other hand, some revisions are made that change the entire significance of the original statement. As an example, consider the following sentence from the first edition.

> Yet in North America there are woodpeckers which feed largely on fruit, and others with elongated wings which chase insects on the wing; and on the plains of La Plata, where not a tree grows, there is a woodpecker, which in every essential part of its organization, even in its colouring, in the harsh tone of its voice, and undulatory flight, told me plainly of its close blood-relationship to our common species; yet it is a wood-pecker which never climbs a tree.[11]

The purpose of describing the woodpecker was to point out to the reader that he had discovered a bird with woodpecker characteristics that does not live as a woodpecker. This purpose becomes untenable as the revisions proceed. By the time the sixth edition is published and all of the concessions are made and embellishments added, we discover that *Colaptes campestris* is after all a rather ordinary woodpecker.

> Yet in North America there are woodpeckers that feed largely on fruit, and others with elongated wings which chase insects on the wing. On the plains of La Plata, where hardly a tree grows [in the fifth edition, he conceded that some trees do grow in the area], there is a woodpecker *(Colaptes capestris)* which has two toes before and two behind, a long pointed tongue, pointed tailfeathers, sufficiently stiff to support the bird in a vertical position on a post, but not so stiff as in the typical woodpecker, and a straight strong beak. The beak, however, is not so straight or strong enough to bore into wood; and I mention, as another illustration of the varied habits of the tribe, that a Mexican *Colaptes* had been described by De Saussure as boring into hard wood in order to lay up a store

of acorns for its future consumption! ["Into hard wood" is changed in the fifth edition to read "into wood" because if the beaks are not as straight or strong as a typical woodpecker, then how can they bore into hard wood? Finally, everything from the last semicolon is removed from the sixth edition.] Hence this *Colaptes* in all the essential parts of its structure is a woodpecker. Even in such trifling characters as the colouring, the harsh tone of its voice, and undulatory flight, its close blood-relationship to our common woodpecker is plainly declared; yet, as I can assert, not only from my own observations, but from those of the accurate Azara [local inhabitants], in certain large districts it does not climb trees, and it makes its nest in holes in banks! [Now he has conceded that the bird does climb trees in some districts.] In certain other districts, however, this same woodpecker, as Mr. Hudson states, frequents trees, and bores holes in the trunk for its nest. [Now we learn that the bird is able to nest in the holes that it is capable of boring.][12]

The reader will note how Darwin attempted to make something significant for evolutionary hypothesis out of *Colaptes campestris*. He was attempting to persuade the reader that he had discovered a bird that was evolving to become a woodpecker. For example, it has stiff tail feathers, but not as stiff as a typical woodpecker; it has a strong beak, but not as strong as a typical woodpecker; it does not climb trees. But in the end, over a span of about 13 years and five editions, it is conceded that there are some trees in La Plata, the bird can climb them, bore holes in them, and nest in them. I have quoted mostly from the first and sixth editions; altogether, it requires an entire page to record the revisions and additions made between the first and sixth editions without repeating original text.

"Of the 3,878 sentences in the first edition, nearly 3,000, about 75 percent, were rewritten from one to five times each."[13] Most of the revisions seem to be nothing more than worrisome tinkering. If one realizes that his hypothesis is not provable by any scientific test and that he himself viewed the book as "one long argument," the tinkering becomes understandable. The thought that may well have been the cause of his obsession with the wording in the *Origin* was the specter that, being an argument, others could argue against it, and being non-provable, it could possibly be subject to disproof. Because the book is essentially an argument, it is inherently biased. The bias lies in the fact that he was arguing for a materialistic explanation for the origin of life, which would complement the new materialism of the age. That being the case, it is obvious that he was not likely to look at any evidence from a creation point of view, since it was that point of view that he was arguing against. This is in contrast to an honest-to-goodness scientific investigation that would attempt to prove how life arose, per se, rather than attempting *a priori* to prove that it arose materialistically.

Eventually Darwin's argument resulted in five revised editions and "over 1,500 sentences being added, and of the original sentences, plus these, nearly 325 were dropped. Of the original and added sentences there were nearly 7,500 variants of all kinds. In terms of net added sentences, the sixth edition is nearly a third as long again as the first."[14] Even spread out over many years, it was a tremendous effort that must have consumed a great deal of time and energy. It also affected his health and was the main cause of his psychoneurosis. One can imagine the daily tension plaguing someone who has written an argument concerning a very controversial issue and the constant concern as to how long his arguments would stand the test of time. Would someone eventually advance a decisive argument against it? Would someone conduct a conclusive test against the hypothesis?

The Technique of Covert Intimidation

The psychology involved in Darwin's method of persuasion is the highlight of the *Origin*. It is the writing style and his unique presentation of evidence, not the "scientific-ness" of the hypothesis, that is the persuasive factor. The skeptical reader is generally mentally unprepared to untangle arguments as intricately woven as those in the *Origin*. One is also confronted with imagination extensively applied, and the critic, thinking in terms of reality, is left with the only recourse, silence, if not acceptance. Even the mechanics of sentence structure, such as the frequent use of semicolons, seem to conspire against the reader. Quite often the essence of a sentence or sentences is difficult or impossible to discover. For example, consider this quote from the *Origin* and comments by Samuel Butler.

"In the earlier editions of this work I underrated, as now seems probable, the frequency and importance of modifications due to spontaneous variability. But it is impossible to attribute to *this cause* [i.e., spontaneous variability, which is itself only an expression for unknown causes] the innumerable structures which are so well adapted to the habits of life of each species. I can no more believe in this [i.e., that the innumerable structures, etc., can be due to unknown causes] than the well adapted form of a racehorse or greyhound, which, before the principle of selection by man was well understood, excited so much surprise in the minds of the older naturalists, can thus [i.e., by attributing them to unknown causes] be explained."

It is impossible to believe that after years of reflection upon his subject, Mr. Darwin should have written as above, especially in such a place, if his mind was clear about his own position. Immediately after the admission of a certain amount of miscalculation there comes a more or less exculpatory sentence, which sounds so right that ninety-nine people out of a hundred would walk through it, unless led by some exigency of their own position to examine it closely, but which yet, upon examination, proves to be as nearly meaningless as a sentence can be.[15]

Darwin often confuses the reader by making an assertion and then obscuring it by qualifying it or appearing to renege. Generally, Darwin followed the rule of using a maximum number of words to establish a minimum number of concepts or ideas, rather than the other way around. Consequently, not everyone has the patience or the mental stamina to read the *Origin* cover to cover. The persuasive, argumentative nature of the *Origin* is described in the reaction of John Stuart Mill.

His first reaction to the book was genuine astonishment that so much could have been done with so fantastic an idea. Darwin had not proved the truth of his hypothesis, but he had proved that it might be true, which Mill took to be "as great a triumph as knowledge and ingenuity could possibly achieve on such a question." Nothing can be at first sight more entirely unplausible than his hypothesis, and yet after beginning by thinking it impossible, one arrives at something like an actual belief in it, and one certainly does not relapse into complete disbelief.[16]

Gertrude Himmelfarb, in *Darwin and the Darwinian Revolution*, describes the *Origin* with uncanny insight.

> It was probably less the weight of the facts than the weight of the argument that was impressive. The reasoning was so subtle and complex as to flatter and disarm all but the most wary intelligence. Only upon close inspection do the faults of the hypothesis emerge. And this close inspection, by the nature of the case, was rarely vouchsafed. The points were so intricately argued that to follow them at all required considerable patience and concentration — an expenditure of effort which was itself conducive to acquiescence. Only those determined in advance to be hostile were likely to maintain a vigilant and hence critical attitude.[17]

Using the length of giraffes' necks as an example, Himmelfarb describes Darwin's technique in more detail.

> The undisciplined nature of Darwin's concept of adaptation may be seen in his reply to those critics who objected that the same process that might be thought to account for the long neck of the giraffe, might also have been expected to produce long necks in other species, the ability to browse upon the high branches of trees being of as much apparent advantage to one quadruped as to another. In a later edition of the *Origin*, Darwin attempted to meet this objection, first by explaining that an adequate answer to this as to so many other questions was impossible because of our ignorance of all the conditions determining the number, range, size and structure of species; and then suggesting possible reasons why the giraffe alone developed a long neck, such as that only in that one species were all of the necessary correlated variations present in precisely the right degree and at the right time. He frankly admitted that these reasons were "general," "vague" and "conjectural." In fact, they were as hypothetical as the hypothesis they were intended to support. There would be no objection

to such hypothetical reasons if they merely served to establish the consistency of the hypothesis. But what they establish is less its consistency than its plasticity, the ease with which it can be bent into any desired shape. If some animals had long necks, Darwin could summon up enough general, vague and conjectural reasons to account for this peculiar fact; if others did not, he had at hand a different but equally general vague and conjectural set of reasons to account for that.

In his rapid volley of explanations, where one might fail, another would hit the mark, and where one line of defense had to be abandoned, another was hastily erected. And there were few to point out that in the strategy of reason, as in the strategy of warfare, the cause was not better served by a succession of feeble defenses than by a single strong one.[18]

Darwin's method of persuasion may be described as covert intimidation. The central component of the method is what Darwin called his golden rule, which was his policy that "whenever a published fact, a new observation or thought came across me, which was opposed to my general results, to make a memorandum of it without fail and at once; for I had found by experience that such facts and thoughts were far more apt to escape from the memory than favourable ones. Owing to this habit, very few objections were raised against my views which I had not at least noticed and attempted to answer."[19]

Of course, any theorist would look for objections or conflicting facts to his hypothesis; it is a perfectly reasonable thing to do, but it is the *spirit* in which it is done that separates Darwin from the exact scientist. The exact scientist is attempting to make a truth statement about the environment and, consequently, is objectively looking for conflicting facts that will reveal his hypothesis as false. What the golden rule accomplished was to place Darwin, at least initially, in an offensive rather than a defensive position, making it possible for him to shift the burden of proof to his critics. It also gives the impression of objectivity rather than bias. One gets the distinct impression when reading the *Origin* that having voluntarily brought up the criticism, and not what he wrote in defense, was sufficient to neutralize it. For example: "Thus a distinguished German naturalist has recently asserted that the weakest part of my theory is that I consider all organic beings as imperfect;

what I really said is that all are not as perfect in relation to the conditions under which they live." The point of the criticism being that, if organisms are imperfect, why have they survived for an indefinite length of time, and if their obvious survival indicates that they are perfect, what is the purpose of evolution? Darwin answered the criticism by simply restating it.

Neutralizing Criticisms

Regarding flatfish, which rest on their sides near the ocean bottom and have both eyes on one side of their head, one critic asked, "If the transit was gradual, then how such transit of one eye a minute fraction of the journey toward the other side of the head could benefit the individual. . . ?"[20] Darwin, apparently unable to answer the criticism through his own hypothesis of natural selection, which is where the criticism was directed, chooses to answer with Jean Lamarck's defunct hypothesis of use and disuse: It is the result of "habit, no doubt beneficial to the individual and to the species, of endeavoring to look upward, with both eyes, whilst resting on one side on the bottom." In other words, attempting to look upward caused one eye to eventually move to the opposite side of the head, and this supposedly became genetically hereditary throughout the species!

Another critic asked: According to natural selection, what advantage would the incipient (partly developed), infinitesimal beginnings be of the twining of tendrils in plants? Darwin answered that he noted that some plants' shoots and leaves moved when repeatedly touched or shaken. And from this observation one can imagine the development of tendrils![21] Himmelfarb elaborates on Darwin's unlimited imagination.

At one point in his autobiography, Darwin objected to the criticism that he was a good observer but a poor reasoner. The *Origin*, he protested with justice, was "one long argument from the beginning to the end" and could only have been written by one with "some power of reasoning." He also remarked that he had a "fair share of inventiveness" — which erred only in being too modest. For his essential method was neither observing, nor the more prosaic mode of scientific reasoning, but a peculiarly imaginative, inventive mode of argument. It was this that Whewell objected to in the *Origin*, for it is assumed that the mere possibility of imagining a series of steps of transition from one condition of organs to another is to be accepted as a reason for believing that such transition has taken place. Such a possibility being thus imagined, we may assume an unlimited number of generations for the transition to take place in, and that this indefinite time may extinguish all doubt that the transitions really have taken place.

What Darwin was doing, in effect, was creating a "logic of possibility." Unlike conventional logic, where the compound of possibilities results not in a greater possibility or probability, but in a lesser one, the logic of the *Origin* was one by which possibilities were assumed to add up to probability.[22]

One can see how a critic, scientifically thinking in terms of reality, is intimidated into silence by conjecture and imagination. A critic could reply with conjecture of his or her own, but that would pointlessly lead nowhere.

The fossil record indicates how Darwin could free his hypothesis from the burden of proof and shift it to the critic. Fossils are the preserved remains of past life, and they should tell the story as to whether or not evolution has occurred. As some present-day evolutionists have acknowledged, the hypothesis fails the prediction that we should find a multitude of intermediate fossils that show evolutionary development from simple to complex. The critic would say that the reason we do not find intermediate fossils is because they never existed; in other words, evolution has not occurred. To answer this difficulty, Darwin speculated that the intermediates did form fossil remains but were later destroyed by natural forces, or we simply have not as yet discovered them.

Now the critic is left in the position of trying to prove a negative — that something the evidence indicates never existed did not leave fossil remains that were later destroyed or that nowhere in the earth's crust a mother lode of intermediate fossils is preserved. According to sound science, we should simply say that Darwin's hypothesis has failed a prediction. Originally, as Darwin's notes from 1837 indicate, he planned on getting out of this difficulty by shifting the burden of proof onto his critics, as follows: "Yes, if you will show me every step between bulldog and greyhound." Obviously, for the sake of sound science, the theorist must assume the responsibility of proof, not the critic.

Sometimes Darwin simply denied the existence of what to everyone else is a conflicting fact. It is in regard to variations that this disagreement occurs: "That a limit to variations does exist in nature is assumed by most authors, though I am unable to discover a single fact on which this belief is grounded."[23] This one statement is a revelation regarding Darwin's determination not to allow anything to stand in the way of his hypothesis. Let us analyze it: "That a limit to variations does exist is assumed by most authors." The obvious reason why most authors assume that variations are limited is because they do not observe dramatic, unlimited variations that would result in new kinds of organisms: ". . . though I am unable to discover a single fact on which this belief is grounded." If unlimited variations were observed, no one would assume limited variations. Limited variations would mean that species are immutable (do not change), which, of course, is a denial of evolutionary hypothesis. Darwin must also have observed limited variations, but, for the sake of his views, he assumed something quite the opposite — unlimited variations.

Essentially, what Darwin was saying in that statement is that we observe limited variations, but perhaps unlimited variations exist although they have not, as yet, been observed. Again the critic has been placed in the position of trying to prove a negative.

Again in relation to variations, we can see how Darwin and Wallace conspire to shift the burden of proof. Darwin stated that useful variations may "occur in the course of thousands of generations." But A.R. Wallace warns Darwin that that statement is too assertive and might favor the critics, so he advises him on a method of which Darwin is already a master: "Such expression gives your opponent the advantage of assuming that favorable variations are rare accidents, or even for long periods may never occur at all and thus [the] argument would appear to many to have great force. I would put the burden of proof on my opponent to show that any one organ, structure, or faculty, does not vary, even during one generation, among all the individuals of a species; and also to show any mode or way, in which any such organs, and so on, does not vary."[24]

It is obvious that the *Origin* is not your typical scientific treatise; rather it is a persuasive argument. The hypothesis does not agree with the facts, and the question of actual proof is not considered. The only thing being tested is Darwin's powers of persuasion; favorable, questionable evidence is magnified in importance, while conflicting facts are discounted as unimportant. William Hopkins' criticism perhaps best exemplifies the true character of Darwin's hypothesis:

> Indeed, our author makes at any time but little use of the verb "to prove," in any of its inflections. His formula is "I am convinced," "I believe," and not "I have proved." We are not finding fault with these more modest forms of expressions; but we may be allowed, perhaps, to remark, that they are the formulae of a creed, and not of a scientific theory.[25]

Perhaps Hopkins' observation explains C.C. Darlington's approval of Darwin's technique of covert intimidation.

> He was able to put his ideas across not so much because of his scientific integrity, but because of his opportunism, his equivocation and his lack of historical sense. Though his admirers will not like to believe it, he accomplished his revolution by personal weakness and strategic talent more than by scientific virtue.[26]

Darlington finds acceptance in the way "Darwin confused the alternatives on all possible occasions. The confusion helped greatly in dealing with untrained opponents who did not notice the blurring of the issue."[27] Darlington was writing in 1959, the centennial year of the first publication of the *Origin*. Apparently convinced that the "myth of creation" had been supplanted by a belief in evolution, he candidly condones Darwin's methods. It does not matter that science has been manipulated and exploited — the end justifies the means.

Darwin's Psychoneurosis

Darwin's health problems are a classic case of mind-body interaction. Symptoms would come and go, intensify, and abate in accordance with the daily events in his life. Living in an unwell condition most of his life, Darwin was ultrasensitive to his daily health condition; consequently, at times he kept a daily health diary and would frequently report about his health in his letters. As a result of these personal accounts as well as accounts by relatives and friends, we have a detailed description of his illness from the time of its inception until his death.

The following description of Darwin's illness is based primarily on two books on the subject — Sir George Pickering's *Creative Malady* and Ralph Colp Jr.'s *To Be an Invalid*. Both authors are trained in medicine and both are agreed that Darwin's illness was an anxiety-caused psychoneurosis. Colp's conclusion is as follows:

> Although his stomach, heart, skin, and cerebral symptoms were nonspecific, the characteristics of these symptoms to fluctuate in intensity, to undergo sudden exacerbations and remissions, and to run an overall course which was essentially nondeteriorative are indicative of psychic (as opposed to organic) causes.[28]

Pickering concluded similarly:

> The case for a psychoneurosis is first that the symptoms suggest it, and, taken in their entirety, they fit nothing else. Second, there is no evidence that any physical signs were ever found as they should have been after forty years of organic disease, and Darwin consulted the best physicians of his day. ... Third, the circumstances precipitating the attacks are right. Fourth, the illness got better towards the end of his life, which is quite unlike organic disease. Lastly, no other diagnosis that has been proposed, or that I can think of, fits all the facts.[29]

Darwin's suffering consisted of a diverse array of symptoms, the very diversity of which indicate anxiety neurosis, one of the most common forms of psychoneurosis. Throughout much of his adult life, Darwin was never free from one or more of the following symptoms, which varied in frequency and intensity according to the daily events in his life: gastric upset, often accompanied by vomiting, headaches, eczema, and what Pickering believes was Da Costa's syndrome, manifesting pain over the heart, breathlessness, palpitations, and giddiness. Da Costa's syndrome was first recognized during the American Civil War. The symptoms are exaggerated by exercise; consequently, many soldiers would fall out of marches and maneuvers, resulting in large numbers on sick call. Yet to forbid exercise or enjoin rest is to cripple these patients and to bring them to a state of partial or complete invalidism. This, Pickering concludes, is what happened to Darwin.

A physician, when confronted with the symptoms of a psycho-neurosis, runs the risk of misdiagnosis. One risk is failing to diagnose organic disease at a stage when it is curable; the other danger is that of treating a psychoneurosis as though it were a disease of the body. Pickering describes the mind-body interaction of a psychoneurosis as follows:

> The symptoms of the psychoneurosis are the patient's own answer to his otherwise intolerable conflict. The range of symptoms is due, of course, to the variety of circumstances in which the casual disturbance, usually associated with fear, arose; and to the great resources of the human mind in effecting conceal-ment [repression] and disguise. [A neurosis may be defined] as a series of sterotyped reactions to problems which the patient has never solved in the past and is still unable to solve in the present. Not a few of the psychoneuroses seem to be an attempt to hide or disguise these problems so that they cannot easily be recognized by the world, or, indeed, by the patient.
>
> The more intense the conflict, the more securely it tends to be hidden in the mind, and the more profound the psycho-neurosis. Unless the doctor can help the patient to detect and resolve that conflict, the psychoneurosis will continue though its symptoms may change.[30]

Daily Influences

Pickering notes the remarkable consistency in the events precipi-tating an attack. Scientific meetings, going out into society, dinner par-ties, having guests in the house precipitate an attack: "So is perfected the routine of Down House, in which everyone is a slave (probably a willing slave) to Darwin's illness. Any infringement of the rules evokes an attack, e.g., his daughter's wedding, and breakfast with Sir James Paget; his father's funeral is not to be attempted."[31]

Both Colp and Pickering note, but cannot explain, Darwin's "choice" of different somatic symptoms: "why, for example, a stress should at one time cause him eczema, at another time cardiac palpita-tions, and at still another time an upset stomach." Darwin "frequently observed that his fits of eczema energized him." Colp speculates that "his eczema, which (at least on some occasions) was caused by his anxiety, then became an anxiety-reducing device: a substitute object of secondary concern onto which he could shift anxiety from objects of primary concern."[32]

In his autobiography, Darwin explained how they had to give up all dinner parties because the excitement caused violent shivering and vomiting attacks. Pickering points out, "Palpitations and breathlessness would scarcely have been an appropriate protest against a dinner party. Vomiting was exactly right."[33]

Pickering's thesis is that Darwin's psychoneurosis had a practical side in that it made him a recluse, which gave him more time to work on his theories. On the other hand, one could argue that the psychoneurosis was debilitating to the point that it interfered with his work. He probably could have accomplished his goals more easily as a vigorous extrovert, which is what he was before beginning work on evolutionary hypothesis. Pickering explains, "What Darwin was afraid of was putting forward a hypothesis which he had come to know was right, but for which anything resembling scientific proof was lacking."[34] Similarly Colp reports "that Darwin's illness cannot be understood without understanding two attributes of Darwin the man: his determination to win acceptance for his evolutionary theory, and his anxieties over the difficulties of proving his theory and over some of its idealogical consequences."[35] Colp explains in more detail.

> [Darwin] was relieved when he obtained evidence which supported his theory and when his theory answered questions about the origin of species. He also suffered illness when some evidence — such as the facts Hooker brought him about the geographic distribution of plants — did not uphold his theory. The more he collected evidence and explored the multitudinous ramifications of natural selection, the more he encountered — along with problems solved — new problems which could not be solved. The unsolved new and old problems caused him to be tortured with obsessional thoughts, and to become (in his words) "tired" in his thoughts and physical actions.[36]

Cessation of the Illness

Both Colp and Pickering report an unusual phenomenon — Darwin's symptoms of psychoneurosis ceased the last decade of his life, from about 1872 until he died. The symptoms reported after 1872 were caused by organic deterioration common to old age.

Colp reported that "the two individuals who knew most about his health and who were his two main nurses — Emma and his servant, Parslow — both observed that during this last decade his overall health had significantly improved." Colp also reported that in the last decade the vomiting ceased and his stomach distress improved so that he was actually able to work more steadily and he apparently did not complain of skin and heart symptoms.[37]

The question is what caused the improved health during Darwin's old age? Both Colp and Pickering agree that Darwin's chronic illness began in 1837, when he began taking notes for the *Origin*, and ceased approximately the last decade of his life. The sixth and last revised edition of the *Origin* was published in 1872, ten years before he died of heart disease. His psychoneurosis began and abated with his work on evolutionary views. We know that his illness was a mind-body interaction. What then happened to improve his mental health and the interacting somatic symptoms?

The classic cure, and perhaps the only cure, for psychoneurosis is to eliminate the cause of the anxiety. The careful reader of the sixth edition of the *Origin* will discover the cure for Darwin's psychoneurosis. The cure could not have been that he stopped revising the *Origin* after 1872, because the anxiety of having his argument refuted, while still not unreservedly accepted by those whom he most wished to acknowledge acceptance, would remain. What happened was that it was no longer necessary to revise the *Origin* because he had accepted the most recent criticisms and abandoned natural selection, his mechanism for evolution.

In the sixth edition, Darwin added a new chapter devoted to the most recent criticisms of his hypothesis. He made one important concession in the 1869 fifth edition and then made further concessions in the sixth edition that were tantamount to abandoning natural selection. The sixth edition indicates that Darwin did not abandon evolution, per se, rather natural selection, the mechanism for evolution. From an anxiety standpoint, this is an interesting distinction. The idea of evolution, having been around since ancient times, did not originate with Darwin. What had given the idea of evolution new life was natural selection — a scientific mechanism for evolution. Prior to Darwin one could only insist that life had evolved; with natural selection, one had a mechanism as to how life had evolved. The idea of natural selection was his responsibility — not the idea of evolution, so it was only necessary to refute natural selection to relieve his anxiety. But hadn't natural selection become synonymous with evolution? Therefore, without the natural selection mechanism there could be no evolution. Darwin overcame this difficulty by shifting the mechanism for evolution to other causes — causes that were not his responsibility, that were known before the first edition of the *Origin* was published, were never seriously considered and today are considered defunct. Incredibly, while most of Western culture came to accept natural selection, the author rejected it.

The Abandonment of Natural Selection

The abandonment of natural selection as the mechanism for evolution began in the fifth edition, published in 1869, and was completed in the sixth edition, published in 1872. St. George Mivart was quick to note "that in early editions of the *Origin* and in the *Descent of Man*, Darwin had relegated it to a subordinate position."[38] The statement errs only in degree — Darwin not only made natural selection subordinate, he set so many limitations upon it that the mechanism was rendered an impossibility.

The first limitation was in response to an anonymous article published in the *North British Review* in 1867. Today we know that the anonymous author was none other than his former ally Asa Gray. Although in his private letters Darwin attributed the authorship of the article to a Fleeming Jenkin, he may well have suspected Asa Gray. The article is written with all of the style and flair so characteristic of Gray's writing.

It is apparent from the following quote that Darwin had undergone a changed attitude toward his hypothesis. Formerly, as we have seen, he would simply deny or not give credit to any criticisms. For example, his view requires unlimited variability, but we observe limited variability. Darwin simply denied that conflicting fact. Or consider the fossil record — his hypothesis predicts numerous intermediate fossils. He simply makes excuses as to why they are not discovered. But in 1869 he admitted to an error in judgment and modified his hypothesis, yet the difficulty was no more severe than limited variability or the lack of intermediate fossils.

It should be observed that, in the above illustration, I speak of the slimmest individual wolves, and not of any single strongly-marked variation having been preserved. In former editions of this work I sometimes spoke as if this latter alternative had frequently occurred. I saw the great importance of individual differences, and this led me fully to discuss the results of unconscious selection by man, which depends on the preservation of all the more or less valuable individuals, and on the destruction of the worst. I saw, also, that the preservation in a state of nature of any occasional deviation of structure, such as a monstrosity, would be a rare event; and that, if at first preserved, it would generally be lost by subsequent intercrossing with ordinary individuals. Nevertheless, until reading an able and valuable article in the *North British Review* (1867), I did not appreciate how rarely single variations, whether slight or strongly-marked, would be perpetuated. The author takes the case of a pair of animals, producing during their lifetime two hundred offspring, of which, from various causes of destruction, only two on an average survive to procreate their kind. This is rather an extreme estimate for most of the higher animals, but by no means so for many of the lower organisms. He then shows that if a single individual were born, which varied in some manner, giving it twice as good a chance of life as that of the other individuals, yet the chances would be strongly against its survival. Supposing it to survive and to breed, and that half its young inherited the favourable variation; still, as the reviewer goes on to show, the young would have only a slightly better chance of surviving and breeding; and this chance would go on decreasing in the succeeding generation. The justice of these remarks cannot, I think, be disputed. If, for instance, a bird of some kind could procure its food more easily by having its beak curved, and if one were born with its beak strongly curved, and which consequently flourished, nevertheless there would be a very poor chance of this one individual perpetuating its kind to the exclusion of the common form; but there can hardly be a doubt, judging by what we see taking place under domestication, that this result would follow from the preservation during many of a large number of individuals with more or less strongly curved beaks, and from the destruction of a still larger number with the straightest beaks.[39]

The limitation for natural selection is the requirement of a large number of similar variations in a population, as opposed to a single variation. This quote remains in the sixth edition. The following quotes tell us how Darwin modified his thinking to fit the previous quote in another part of the *Origin*. The critical words are italicized.

Third edition: The fact of little or no modification having been effected since the glacial period would be of some avail against those who believe in the existence of an innate and necessary law of development, but is powerless against the doctrine of natural selection, which only implies that *variations occasionally occurring in single species are under favourable conditions preserved.*

As we shall learn, "single species" means a single member of a species:

Fourth edition: . . . which implies only *that variations occasionally occur in single species*, and that these when favourable are preserved; but this will occur only at long intervals of time after changes in the condition of each country.

Now in the fifth edition he modifies the sentence and changes single to a few members of a species in order to accommodate his error in judgment.

Fifth edition: . . . Selection or the survival of the fittest, which implies only that *variations or individual differences of a favourable nature* occasionally arise in a few [obviously a few members of a species] species and are then preserved.

Finding himself boxed in on the number of variations required — a single variation being insufficient, a few probably inadequate, and to require a large number of similar variations to suddenly appear in a population is really a form of creation, Darwin disguises the issue in the sixth edition.

Sixth edition: . . . implies that when variations or individual differences of a beneficial nature happen to arise, these will be preserved; but this will be effected only under certain favorable circumstances.[40]

More Limitations

The following limitation for natural selection to be effective was added to the sixth edition and seems not to be a reaction to a criticism, but rather a limitation voluntarily added by Darwin. The significant words are italicized.

It may be well to remark that with all beings there must be much fortuitous destruction, which can have little or no influence on the course of natural selection. For instance, a vast number of eggs or seeds are annually devoured and these could be modified through natural selection only if they varied in some manner which protected them from their enemies. Yet many of these eggs of seeds would perhaps, if not destroyed, have yielded individuals better adapted to their conditions of life than any of those which happen to survive. So again a vast number of mature animals and plants, whether by accidental causes, which would not be in the least degree mitigated by certain changes of structure or constitution, would in other ways be beneficial to the species. But let the destruction of the adults be ever so heavy, if the number which can exist in any district be not wholly kept down by such causes, or again let the destruction of eggs or seeds be so great that only a hundredth of a thousandth part are developed — yet of those that survive, the best adapted individuals, supposing that there is any variability in a favourable direction, will tend to propagate their kind in larger numbers than the less well adapted. If *the numbers be wholly kept down by the causes just indicated, as will often be the case, natural selection will be powerless in certain beneficial directions*; but this is no valid objection to its efficiency at other times and in other ways; for we are far from having any reason to suppose that many species ever undergo modification and improvement at the same time in the same area.[41]

The last sentence clearly states that natural selection is ineffective when populations are not growing, but then, as is often the case, he seems to renege on the assertion after the first semicolon, but does not elaborate. The new limitation added to natural selection — that populations must be growing and must have numerous similar variations to select upon — makes the validity of the mechanism doubtful and reveals Darwin's weakened resolve to defend the hypothesis against all criticisms.

Finally, also in the sixth edition, Darwin makes another concession that destroys natural selection. This is in response to the criticism that there is no survival advantage in rudimentary or incipient (partly developed) organs. As described previously, what survival advantage could there be in the first minute movement of the eye of a flatfish to the opposite side of the head, or the beginning of twining in plants, or for that matter, the beginning development of any organ? For an organ to convey a survival advantage, it would have to come into existence fully functional. Mr. Mivart's objection is that natural selection would be ineffective in preserving incipient organs since they would not be of any advantage until fully developed. Darwin considered several of these cases and concluded as follows:

> I have now considered enough, perhaps more than enough, of the cases, selected with care by a skilful naturalist, *to prove that natural selection is incompetent to account for the incipient stages of useful structures;* and I have shown, as I hope, that there is no great difficulty on this head. [Italics added]

And again:

> The belief that any given structure, which we think, often erroneously, would have been beneficial to a species, would have been gained under all circumstances through natural selection, is opposed to what we can understand of its manner of action.[42]

Incredibly, Darwin sided with Mivart against natural selection to prove its incompetence. That spells the end of natural selection, the mechanism that was his contribution to evolutionary views and the center of focus for his anxiety. The entire idea of natural selection was the belief that it could bring into existence new organs and organisms through insensibly slow and minute steps; the idea of simple to complex. Natural selection was the alternative to creation, the belief that organisms came into existence fully developed by supernatural power.

Does Darwin's denial of natural selection as a creative mechanism make it completely nonfunctional? Possibly not. The possibility exists that natural selection may be a viable, but noncreative, mechanism in regard to slight differences in fully functional structures under certain environmental circumstances. He does continue to mention natural selection but makes light of its creative potential.

I was pleased to discover that the analysis that I had been making of the revisions of the sixth edition of the *Origin* and my conclusion that Darwin had abandoned natural selection as a creative mechanism is verified by Darwin in a source other than the *Origin* itself. I am referring to a letter to the editor written by Darwin in *Nature, A Weekly Illustrated Journal of Science* in 1880 that would make it approximately eight years after the sixth edition of the *Origin* was published and approximately two years prior to his death. Darwin responded to the following quote by Sir Wyville Thomson: "The character of the abyssal fauna [animal life deep in the ocean depths] refuses to give the least support to the theory which refers the evolution of species to extreme variation guided only by natural selection." Rather than defending natural selection, the idea to which he owed his fame and that had become synonymous with evolution in the public mind, he demoted it: "Can Sir Wyville Thomson name any one who has said that the evolution of species depends only on natural selection?" Remember, until the sixth edition, natural selection was the exclusive mechanism for evolution. He continues the letter by pointing out that he was the foremost promoter of use and disuse of parts as a means of evolution: "As far as concerns myself, I believe that no one has brought forward so many observations on the effects of the use and disuse of parts, as I have done in my *Variation of Animals and Plants under Domestication;* and these observations were made for this special object."[43]

With the abandonment of natural selection, he had freed himself from his mental imprisonment to a cause and idea that he no longer needed. The hypothesis had provided him with fame and recognition, but at this stage in his life he preferred peace of mind.

The reader will note in the quotation pertaining to incipient stages that Darwin seems to again renege by stating, "I hope that there is no great difficulty on this head," when there is the utmost difficulty for natural selection. In this case, what he apparently means is that the reader may continue to believe in evolution, but will have to accept something other than his natural selection as the mechanism. What other mechanisms did he consider? The following quotations are in the sixth edition only.

> There is another possible mode of transition, namely, through the acceleration or retardation of the period of reproduction. . . . In all such cases — and many could be given — if the age for reproduction were retarded, the character of the species, at least in its adult state, would in some cases be hurried through and finally lost.[44]

Organisms do not reproduce until maturity, but Darwin, having no knowledge of genetics, assumes that reproducing early or late in maturity would somehow result in different offspring. The following sentence originated in the first edition of the *Origin*.

> I have now recapitulated the facts and considerations which have thoroughly convinced me that species have been modified during a long course of descent by the preservation or the natural selection of many successive slight favourable variations.

The sentence was continued as follows in the sixth edition.

> . . . aided in an important manner by the inherited effects of the use and disuse of parts; and in an unimportant manner, that is in relation to adaptive structure, whether past or present, by the direct action of external conditions, and by variations which seem to us in our ignorance to arise spontaneously.

In analyzing the sentence, we find that Lamarck's defunct hypothesis of use and disuse of parts (also mentioned in Darwin's letter to the editor) is considered an important method of change. The direct action of external conditions, whatever that means, is considered unimportant. Finally, he considers spontaneous change (i.e., change without a natural mechanism, which is somewhat like describing creation) as also being a mode of transition. He concluded with the following statement:

> It appears that I formerly underrated the frequency and value of these latter forms of variation, as leading to permanent modifications of structure independently of natural selection.[45]

The irony of all this is that it has become standard procedure in high school biology textbooks to present the hypothesis of use and disuse of parts, originated by the French naturalist Jean Lamarck in 1801, as a defunct hypothesis by comparing it to Darwin's natural selection. In other words, Darwin abandoned his own natural selection mechanism in favor of what was then and now considered an obsolete theory. Lamarck explained, for example, that giraffes needed a long neck for feeding in trees and that by stretching their necks, the trait was hereditarily passed on to their offspring. In textbooks, this is usually explained with a series of pictures of giraffes.

It is rare among scientists to admit to a mistaken hypothesis; Darwin was an exception. Usually a hypothesis becomes obsolete by attrition, as its supporters die off and no new proponents are generated. Darwin had the extenuating circumstances of his illness with which to contend, yet his abandonment of natural selection appears to be subversive by making it subsidiary to other mechanisms and by setting limits that make it a physical impossibility. Perhaps it was not as subversive as it appears.

Although revisions in the *Origin* tell us that Darwin relieved his anxiety by refuting natural selection as a creative mechanism, which was his main contribution to evolutionary hypothesis, while promoting Lamarck's idea of use and disuse as an evolutionary mechanism, the possibility exists that privately he may have rejected the whole idea of organic evolution as opposed to special creation. I am basing this possibility upon a pamphlet that has been widely circulated among creationists for many years and the fact that he shifted emphasis to Lamarck's hypothesis, which was not seriously considered even in his day. The pamphlet to which I am referring describes an incident when a Lady Hope visited Darwin, who was bedridden, shortly before his death. During the course of the conversation, the Book of Genesis was alluded to, whereupon Darwin became greatly distressed and supposedly commented as follows: "I was a young man with unformed ideas. I threw out queries, suggestions, wondering all the time over everything; and to my astonishment the ideas took like wildfire. People made a religion of them."[46]

It would require an enormous amount of courage to publicly reject the whole idea of organic evolution, which would have generated widespread ridicule. On the other hand, rejecting natural selection, that which he had made synonymous to evolutionary hypothesis, and including it among the verbiage of the sixth edition was enough to cure his psychoneurosis. He was not anxiety-ridden enough to go beyond that; it was sufficient to extricate him from the whole affair.

Considering the circumstances of his time, perhaps Darwin deserves credit for being quite courageous. When one stops to think about it, his abandonment of natural selection was rather straight-forward and scientific. It wasn't as though he blindly recanted because of a religious belief. He plainly states in the sixth edition that he agrees with the author of the article in the *North British Review* that natural selection would require numerous similar variations to suddenly occur in a population. In other words, natural selection would require a super-natural or supranatural input before it could become effective, making the mechanism superfluous. He also plainly states in the sixth edition that he agrees with Mivart that natural selection cannot account for the development of incipient organs. That in itself is enough to strip the natural selection mechanism of any creative potential. The only thing left for natural selection is that of a "conservative rather than a creative force."[47] As you shall read, that was the original concept of natural selection as proposed by Edward Blyth.

The problem was not Darwin's lack of courage. Rather it was the blindness of the proponents of evolution. Too many people suddenly jumped on the evolutionary bandwagon; the social Darwinists too rapidly integrated the hypothesis into Western culture, and the theo-logians prematurely incorporated it into their theology. Darwin's aban-donment of natural selection was not for his generation, but for ours.

Somehow, it all has the ring of a grotesque joke upon society. While Darwinian evolution became incorporated into our culture, the author was abandoning his mechanism for evolution in favor of use and disuse, which, Darwin was well aware, would fail to gain acceptance.

Why Darwin Abandoned Natural Selection

One may speculate widely as to why Darwin, in his old age, abandoned natural selection. On the surface it seems incongruous that he would concede defeat in the face of an overwhelming victory in terms of widespread public acceptance. Why did he allow Mivart's and Gray's criticisms to carry so much weight? Why not simply deny the validity of their criticism as, in the other cases, he had so often done previously? One possibility may be that, after so many years of defending his hypothesis, they were simply the straws that broke the camel's back. I am convinced that Mivart's and Gray's criticisms were actually, at that stage in his life, viewed as an opportunity to extricate himself from an increasingly intolerable situation.

By 1872, Darwin may have recognized a phenomenon of which few people today are aware regarding public acceptance of evolutionary hypothesis, namely, that its success was primarily through the efforts of the social Darwinists, rather than its scientific validity. We have already learned how Darwin's hypothesis, in the form of the concepts of progress and survival of the fittest, had permeated every aspect of Western culture from theology to sociology. With all of that going for it, the scientific validity of the hypothesis was seldom questioned by the public or for that matter by scientists themselves. But to Darwin it remained the paramount question in his life. Darwin's persuasion tactics had given him a shallow, tenuous victory in the public view, but not among those in science whom he wished most to convince. The possibility exists that evolutionary views may have been, in Darwin's mind, a dismal failure. At one point Darwin expressed the opinion that he would consider his hypothesis a success if he could persuade one competent judge. Not the social Darwinists or the general public, but someone in science and most especially a personal acquaintance, such as Huxley, Gray, Hooker, or Lyell. Some of these people encouraged Darwin to publish, yet none of them would publicly endorse evolutionary views without reservations.

We have learned how Darwin had a falling out with Asa Gray, who endorsed theistic evolution. Even Joseph Hooker, his closest friend, made his reservations known. Then there is Thomas Huxley, who avidly promoted the hypothesis but was careful to protect himself by describing its failings, perhaps on a less enthusiastic scale. I believe that the success or failure of Darwin's life work centered on whether or not the prestigious Sir Charles Lyell would unreservedly endorse evolutionary views. There was something about Lyell that awed Darwin; perhaps it was Lyell's own success in uniformitarian geology, which was an integral part of his own hypothesis, that made him the one person in the world he most wanted to persuade. The following excerpts indicate that Darwin needed Lyell's endorsement in order to persuade the public, but the hypothesis had caught on regardless of Lyell's wholehearted acceptance of the hypothesis as his own personal indicator of success.

On September 2, 1859, prior to the publication of the first edition, Darwin wrote to Lyell: "Remember, your verdict will probably have more influence than my book in deciding whether such views as I hold will be admitted or rejected at present; in the future, I cannot doubt about their admittance."[48] But, "Lyell could not give up creation, especially the separate creation of man. Therefore, he could not declare himself openly a convert to natural selection."[49] On February 25, 1860, Darwin wrote, "I cannot help wondering at your zeal about my book. I declare to heaven you seem to care as much about my book as I do myself."[50] Although Darwin was led to believe that in Lyell's *Antiquity of Man* or in a later edition of the *Principles of Geology* he would publicly declare his conversion, the leap of faith was never made. On July 18, 1867, eight years after the first edition was published and after it was apparent that the hypothesis was gaining public acceptance, Darwin still longed for Lyell's endorsement and wrote to him as follows: "I rejoice in my heart that you are going to speak out plainly about species."[51] Finally, his letters began to express bitterness: "I have been greatly disappointed that you have not given judgment and spoken fairly out what you think about the derivation of species. . . . I think the *Parthenon* is right, that you will lead the public in a fog. . . . I had always thought that your judgment would have been an epoch in the subject. All that is over with me, and I will only think on the admirable skill with which you have selected striking points."

Lyell replied, "You ought to be satisfied, as I shall bring hundreds towards you who, if I treated the matter more dogmatically, would have rebelled."

Darwin could by no means be satisfied. He went as far as courtesy would permit in suggesting to Lyell that his treatment of the species question was not honest: "It is nearly as much for your sake as for my own that I so much wish that your state of belief would have permitted you to say boldly and distinctly out that species were not separately created."[52]

Dupree reports on the fellowship shared by Gray and Lyell for not converting to Darwin's belief on evolution: "Thus at a series of dinner parties, after Sir Charles had reached the age of seventy, two of the original Darwinians celebrated both their community of interest in the fact that they formed a minority rejected by the reigning priests of Darwinism. The cliché was already well formed that *On the Origin of Species* had killed the argument of Paley, but two men whose contributions to the evolutionary movement outshone almost everyone's save Darwin himself could still trust their faith in an ordered world of nature. It was a melancholy satisfaction for Gray to know that his line had been followed by the great Lyell."[53]

It is comical, in a way, that while Gray waited impatiently for Darwin to announce his acceptance of theistic evolution, Darwin was anxiously waiting for Lyell to announce his acceptance of evolutionary views.

The Parallel-roads Incident

A traumatic incident occurred in Darwin's life that most writers only mention in passing. It was an incident that must have left an indelible impression in Darwin's mind, and may have influenced his decision to abandon natural selection half a lifetime later. The incident to which I refer concerns Darwin's abortive attempt to explain the cause of the so-called parallel roads at Glen Roy in the Scottish Highland.

This unusual geological formation, which actually looks like roads or terraces built into sloping land, had been the object of much theorizing for some time. Assuming that water could not have been dammed back by rocks, Darwin concluded that the terraces were ancient sea beaches raised to their present level by a gradual elevation of the land. This hypothesis was not a true hypothesis at the outset (a true hypothesis being one that agrees with all of the facts) because it was contradicted by the absence of seashells that it predicts should be found. But that did not deter Darwin. In a letter to Lyell he reported, "I have fully convinced myself (after some doubting at first) that the shelves are sea beaches although I could not find a trace of a shell; and I think I can explain away most, if not all, the difficulties."[54] His paper was presented before the Royal Society in 1839. One year later two geologists, Agassiz and Burkland, discovered a more plausible explanation in the hypothesis that glaciers had dammed back the water that shaped the terraces.

The reader will note the extraordinary similarity, a forewarning of events to come, between Darwin's parallel-roads hypothesis and his evolution hypothesis. The parallel-roads hypothesis failed the prediction to discover seashells as the evolution hypothesis failed its prediction to discover intermediate fossils.

Imagine the embarrassing trauma Darwin suffered over this incident and only two years after he had begun formulating his evolutionary hypothesis. He was given the opportunity to read the paper before the prestigious Royal Society only to have it refuted shortly afterward. Not having experienced it, we do not fully realize the devastating effect the incident may have had on Darwin, a man who was attempting to make a name for himself in science. I am convinced that this traumatic incident may have caused Darwin to hesitate about publishing the *Origin* and contributed to his psychoneurosis. The more his hypothesis gained in public acceptance, the more fearful he became that it would be refuted and this time the embarrassment would be many times greater than the parallel-roads incident.

Darwin's Plagiarism

Although Darwin read and took notes extensively, the *Origin* was not documented as is the usual practice then and now; consequently, a reader is left with the impression that all of the ideas contained in the *Origin* originated in the mind of Darwin. Such was not the case, although Darwin seemed to be trying to impress the reader that it was when in the first edition he continually referred to the hypothesis as "my theory." The entire book is plagiarized except for covert intimidation, his method of presenting the ideas. Perhaps trying to soothe his conscience, Darwin stated that credit should go to him who succeeds in establishing an idea.

King-Hele described how every topic on which Charles wrote, except a book on *Cirripeda* (barnacles), had been mapped out beforehand in the works of his grandfather, Erasmus. Not only did Charles choose the topics from the works of Erasmus (as an example, King-Hele notes the similarities of Erasmus's version of sexual selection as compared to Charles's), the phraseology is also quite similar: ". . . the pages on evolution in *Zoonomia* abound in sentences of the form: 'when we consider example 1; when we compare X with Y; when we think over example 2; we cannot but conclude that'; and this is one of Charles Darwin's favorite ways of presenting his argument."[55]

Nora Barlow, granddaughter of Charles, summarizes the similarity in topics among the works of Erasmus and Charles: "In *Zoonomia*, Erasmus considers the twining and other movements in plants; the cross-fertilization in plants; the origin of the sense of beauty in connection with the female form; adaptive and protective coloration, heredity, and the domestication of animals. Charles Darwin deals with these subjects in the following books: *Climbing Plants; Power of Movement of Plants; Cross and Self-fertilization in Plants; Fertilization in Plants; Fertilization of Orchids; Descent of Man; Variation of Animals and Plants under Domestication;* and *On the Origin of Species.*"[56]

The actual phrase "natural selection" may have been plagiarized from Patrick Matthews's book, *On Naval Timber and Arboriculture,* which fully anticipates the idea of natural selection. Eiseley, in his book, *Darwin and the Mysterious Mr. X,* provides evidence that Darwin was aware of Matthews by 1844. The man featured as the mysterious Mr. X in Eiseley's book is Edward Blyth, a zoologist. Eiseley reports, "In the British *Magazine of Natural History* in 1835 and again in 1837 — the very year that Darwin opened his first notebook upon the species question — Blyth discussed what today we would call both natural and sexual selection."[57] In this case also, Eiseley provides considerable evidence that Darwin had read Blyth's articles.

Blyth's concept of natural selection was directly opposite that of Darwin. Blyth envisioned natural selection as a "conservative rather than a creative force."[58] Blyth had observed that organisms were well adapted to survive in their environment and any deviation from the norm would decrease rather than increase chances for survival. Eiseley also notes, "The term natural selection has a peculiar history. Under other names it was known earlier within the century, but this is little realized."[59]

The whole purpose of evolutionary hypothesis is to provide a naturalistic explanation for origins as opposed to a supernatural explanation; therefore, the mechanism for origins must be discovered in nature. I am inclined to think that the idea of natural selection was fully developed in Darwin's mind prior to his having read Blyth's articles. What had him stymied was how to present the idea in a convincing manner. Scientifically, the problem could be resolved by observing natural selection in action in the environment, but this he was unable to do. This is confirmed in the *Origin* where he found it necessary to give imaginary examples.

What Darwin may have discovered in Blyth's articles was not the idea of natural selection, but a method for arguing for natural selection, namely, Blyth's use of the natural-selection/artificial-selection analogy. Eiseley reports, "Blyth, long before Darwin had expressed himself on the same subject, had clearly recognized the analogy between artificial and natural selection."[60] What Darwin conceived in Blyth's analogy was a way to overcome the lack of observation of his alleged natural selection. In the *Origin*, Darwin succeeded in making artificial selection the mental stand-in for natural selection. If the reader would believe that humans can select and preserve slight variations among domesticated plants and animals, and who does not believe that, then they should also believe that nature can do likewise. This mental sleight-of-hand is the crowning achievement of his technique of covert intimidation and is quite obvious in the *Origin* once a reader is aware of it. Darwin had subverted Blyth's views of both natural selection and the natural-selection/artificial-selection analogy in order to achieve his own ends, which is probably why Blyth's work was never acknowledged by Darwin.

Darwin's plagiarism and the dishonesty of his persuasion tactics are just two more causes for his anxiety and guilt. The reasons for Darwin's psychoneurosis, as it relates to his views of evolution, seem to be as varied and numerous as the symptoms of his illness. The problem was that he had not conducted a legitimate scientific investigation in which he could rest in comfort no matter what the conclusion.

Who Was Charles Darwin?

Darwin was not the great scientist that he is often made out to be by the scientific community. He was, as the next essay describes, a natural philosopher, not an exact scientist. He was, as others have commented, a good observer but a poor reasoner. Darwin lacked the one attribute required of great scientists — total objectivity. In his autobiography, Darwin described the *Origin* as one long argument from the beginning to the end; consequently, it was a foregone conclusion that he would not be objective. The game was to disguise his lack of objectivity in what was really a persuasive argument. He succeeded in persuading large numbers of people who were perhaps already predisposed to accept evolution. He also succeeded in creating his own little hell on earth by developing an anxiety state that made him a mental and emotional prisoner to his hypothesis, a prison from which he was able to escape only for the last ten years of his life. Darwin's hypothesis has had worldwide ramifications, yet it was all so personal — a struggle between a man's conscience and his vanity.

Finally, for those who are interested in prophecy, T.H. Huxley, at the close of *Darwiniana*, published in 1896, prophesied as to the approximate duration of the influence of Darwin's hypothesis, as though recognizing it as a product of his time.

> I believe that, if you take it as the embodiment of an hypothesis, it is destined to be the guide of biological and psychological speculation for the next three or four generations.[61]

The dictionary estimates 30 years for a generation; that would bring us to right about now.

The Truth about the Evolution Curriculum

One central truth transcends all others regarding the secondary school evolution curriculum. In 1871 St. George Mivart, an acquaintance of Charles Darwin, published a book entitled *On the Genesis of Species* in which he pointed out a fatal flaw in Darwin's hypothetical natural selection mechanism:

> Natural selection utterly fails to account for the conservation and development of the minute rudimentary beginnings, the slight and infinitesimal commencement of structures, however useful those structures may afterward become.[62]

In other words, if natural selection cannot account for the origin of an organ before it has a use, it cannot account for the existence of functional organs later. According to the evolution scenario, all organs would have to begin as incipient structures. Asa Gray explained it this way:

Admitting, therefore, that natural selection may improve organs already useful to great numbers of species, does not imply an admission that it can create or develop new organs, and originate species.[63]

Asa Gray was a Harvard professor of botany and a contemporary of Darwin, which indicates to me that the incipiency problem has always been common knowledge throughout the science establishment, but has been deliberately withheld from the public. The following year Darwin responded to Mivart in the sixth and final edition of the *Origin of Species* with this comment:

I have now considered enough, perhaps more than enough, of the cases selected with care by a skilful naturalist to prove that natural selection is incompetent to account for the incipient stages of useful structures; and I hope that there is no great difficulty on this head.[64]

Amazingly, the quote reads as though Darwin is eager to take credit for proving the incompetence of his own mechanism. But what about the last part of the final clause? It reads as though natural selection's inability to overcome incipiency is no problem, which does not make sense. It reads like some kind of double talk. But, if one carefully reads pages around the quote in question, one gets the drift. In those pages one will find Darwin grasping at straws in an attempt to rescue his belief in evolution by suggesting other methods for evolution. For example, he suggests a vague "variations without selection," the possibility that even the incipient stages are somehow useful, and Jean Lamarck's idea of use and disuse, which means if an organism needs an adaptation or does not need an adaptation it will somehow come into existence or go out of existence. Lamarck's idea of use and disuse was once used in textbooks as an example of a defunct mechanism, which was then supposed to bolster the credibility of natural selection in the minds of students. Darwin, on the other hand, in his desperation to save the evolution belief, was compelled to endorse Lamarck's mechanism over natural selection! Darwin elaborated on his abandonment of natural selection with this statement:

Even if the fitting variations (mutations) did arise, it does not follow that natural selection would be able to act on them, and produce a structure, which apparently would be beneficial to the species.[65]

Mivart disproved natural selection not by experimentation or observation but by critical thinking. Natural selection is incompetent because Darwin was incompetent as a critical thinker. We need go no further because without a viable mechanism there can be no evolution and that means the entire evolution curriculum is discredited. By the way, after the publication of his book, Mivart was ostracized from the inner circle of Darwin supporters. But a mystery remains that we must address.

After owning up to the incipiency problem, Darwin continued in the book as though the problem did not exist. It was as though by simply responding to the fatal flaw it somehow disappeared. It apparently did disappear, from his mind at least and from the minds of evolutionists to follow. What kind of irrational mindset would permit that kind of denial? A denial is possible if evolution exists in one's mind as a theory in name only, but in reality, as a religious doctrine, it is a doctrine with the mission to advance an atheistic world view. To Darwin, the evangelist, the credibility of evolution is not central to his personal belief in an atheistic world view. Evolution is merely the medium by which an atheistic world view is evangelized to others, and to them it must appear to possess at least a modicum of credibility. To make evolution believable to students, it cannot be held accountable as a theory because those standards would ruin its credibility. That is why evolutionists today, taking their cue from Darwin, do not practice objective science and why their brand of science will be corrected in the following pages.

This book introduces four concepts not found in textbooks that cast additional light on the origins issue: The earth's origins evidence is public domain, meaning no one can claim exclusive ownership of evidence and impose their interpretations on everyone else. The earth's origins evidence is everyone's heritage to interpret as they please. Origins research is metaphysical rather than practical. Darwin's investigative method was authoritative rather than legitimate science, and all explanations for origins, including evolution, have religious imperatives.

Darwin Disassociates His Research from Legitimate Science

The evolution idea and objective science are incompatible. We have already learned that natural selection's incipiency problem renders it untenable as the creative mechanism for Darwin's evolution belief. Now we will reveal how Darwin deliberately determined not to hold evolution accountable to objective science.

In order to qualify evolution as a scientific theory, one would have to include alternative points of view for each item of evolution evidence, something evolution proponents, beginning with Darwin himself, have studiously avoided. In addition, all evidence unfavorable to evolution would have to be included. Then and only then can evolution be labeled a theory. The truth is, students believe they are being taught a theory when in reality the prevailing dogma that constitutes evolution research and the evolution curriculum has all the earmarks of an unquestionable religious doctrine. Being a student advocate, I regard the deception a violation of their academic freedom and an abuse of authority by those responsible for the evolution curriculum format. Students are blissfully unaware and youthfully ignorant that evolution dogmatists are taking advantage of their trust. In any other kind of investigation the deliberate withholding of information results in censure. But evolution proponents, concealed behind a banner of scientific objectivity, subject students to a blatant indoctrinating belief in evolution and do it with impunity. The harsh reality is that theories are tentative explanations for phenomena and exist to be overthrown, if possible. That explains why evolution is labeled a theory, which allows access into science classrooms, but the evidence is presented as unquestionable dogma in the typical curriculum. Evolution should be taught as the theory it is purported to be or not at all. The typical evolution curriculum is not scientifically objective because it does not include counterinduction: alternative points of view for each item of evolution evidence. Doctrines abhor counterinduction because it tends to enhance skepticism. Theories, on the other hand, embrace counterinduction because it nurtures skepticism. Evolution, as the textbooks present it, is not true science at all.

The textbook evolution curriculum does not challenge the evidence and therein lies the Gordian knot for evolution dogmatists. Introducing counterinduction into the curriculum would qualify evolution as a theory, but, at the same time, it allows students to directly or indirectly consider alternative explanations for origins relative to the evidence. Obviously, that would seriously weaken the credibility of evolution and undermine its religious mission to advance an atheistic world view. That is why Darwin could not include counterinduction in his research, as he makes known in the introduction to the *Origin*:

> For I am well aware that scarcely a single point is discussed in this volume on which facts cannot be adduced, often leading to conclusions directly opposite to those at which I have arrived. A fair result can be obtained only by fully stating and balancing the facts and arguments on both sides of each question; and this cannot possibly be here done.[66]

Here is a case in point as to why Darwin had no other choice than to do biased research. Evolution proponents claim to have fossil evidence of human evolution, which fits their belief in a materialistic explanation for origins. There is no way to prove that explanation of the fossils. Counterinductively, the scientifically minded skeptic could say that the fossils represent extinct species of primates or races of human beings and have nothing to do with an alleged evolution process. There is no way to prove that explanation either, but it is a fact that extinctions are known to have occurred.

Here is the overall problem Darwin faced regarding nearly all of the evidence. Darwin's evolution explanations are extraordinary while the skeptic's explanations are ordinary. Darwin must have realized that if he allowed counterinduction the reader would most likely choose ordinary over extraordinary explanations.

Darwin's admission of bias is very cleverly written. He admits to doing biased research and then declares himself innocent because it is impossible to be unbiased. An unwary reader may fall for the impossibility excuse, but, as everybody knows, what Darwin deemed to be impossible is an absolute necessity in science investigations. It is no exaggeration to say that Darwin's admission of bias disqualifies his research as legitimate science, but he proceeded anyway, while the science establishment looked the other way. Darwin's concern, which makes sense of the quote, was that it is impossible to write a convincing evolution scenario, if alternative points of view are to be considered. The alternative points of view would directly or indirectly include other religions, to the detriment of his religion. Darwin's use of the word "impossible," or his variation thereof, does not mean counterinduction is impossible but that it is impossible to evangelize evolution with counterinduction. His biased research is really disguised religion. And that is how and why students are denied academic freedom when evolution is taught. Academic freedom is sacrificed in order to mollify evolution's inherent bigotry. Here is how real science advocates contradict Darwin:

> Therefore the first step in our criticism of customary concepts and customary reactions is to step outside the circle and either to invent a new conceptual system, for example, a new theory that clashes with the most carefully established observational results and confounds the most plausible theoretical principles, or to import such a system from outside science from religion, from theology, from the ideas of incompetents, or the ramblings of mad men. This first step is, again counterinductive. Counterinduction is thus both a fact — science could not exist without it — and a legitimate and much needed move in the game of science.[67]

Popper concurs:

> Investigators must . . . try again and again to formulate the theories which they are holding and to criticize them. And try to construct alternative theories — alternatives even to those theories, which occur to you inescapable, for only in that way will you understand the theories you hold. Whenever a theory appears to you as the only possible one, take that as a sign that you have neither understood the theory nor the problem which it was intended to solve.[68]

The evolution curriculum is supposed to be taught according to Popper and Feyerabend, not according to Darwin's misrepresentation of science. It is apparent from the quote that Darwin was setting himself up as a thought dictator on the subject of evolution. In order to formulate a credible evolution scenario, only his opinions regarding the evidence could be taken into consideration. All critical thinking by others would be ignored and suppressed. The type of science that Darwin was advocating is obviously authoritarianism. Authoritarianism does not include counterinduction and experimentation. Instead, explanations for phenomena are accepted on the basis of blind trust in the investigator's expertise. The difference between Darwin and authoritarianism of old is that the latter did not know any better, while Darwin admits that alternative explanations are possible but does not consider them.

Most tenth graders would read Darwin's strategy for making evolution credible and scoff at it as not representing legitimate science. So why does the science establishment allow it? We have to recall that the *Origin* was published when the great scientific and industrial revolution was in full swing. Numerous strides were made in communications, transportation, medicine, and manufacturing; as a result, lives were changed dramatically. Apparently, a clique existed in the science establishment who wanted the crowning achievement, to enter the realm of religion and provide the masses with a scientific, materialistic explanation for origins. Think how that would enhance the prestige of the science establishment. But in order for the science establishment to endorse the *Origin*, it would be necessary to lower their investigative standards to that of Darwin. That is why the *Origin* is with us today as a throwback to primitive science and an insult to objective science.

The question of origins is the seminal question for perhaps all religions, so teaching the earth's origins evidence, which is public domain, from the point of view of one chosen explanation for origins to the exclusion of all others should constitute a violation of the constitutional principle of freedom of religion. One must assume that all explanations for origins, emanating from any sources whatsoever, have religious imperatives behind them.

Attempt to Initiate a Scientifically Objective Evolution Curriculum

I taught a scientifically objective evolution curriculum for many years, during which time no parent or student ever complained. On average, I taught biology to 140 students per year. I taught the textbook evolution curriculum for several years, at the beginning of my career, but after becoming aware that the textbook presentation is unabashed dogmatism, I began to modify the curriculum. This was before I read Darwin's admission to doing biased research in the *Origin of Species*. I could not in good conscience — both personally and professionally — ever go back to teaching textbook evolution dogmatism. To my way of thinking, it meant inconsiderately treating students as mere pawns by the powers that be, in their zeal to evangelize an evolution belief. I was determined to treat students, regardless of the personal beliefs they brought into the classroom, as a thinking class of people who must be made privy to all of the pros and cons about evolution; only then would I be teaching theory rather than doctrine. This meant providing alternative explanations for each item of evolution evidence.

At the outset of the course, the teacher must classify the evolution evidence according to quality. This orients students as to the direction the curriculum will take. For example, geographic distribution, comparative embryology, comparative anatomy, vestigial organs, and the fossil evidence for alleged human evolution are classified as untestable/circumstantial evidence, which means they are poor quality and wide open to counterinduction. The textbooks, on the other hand, would have students believe that all of the evolution evidence is unquestionable. The fossil record would be classified as testable evidence.

After providing an example of an alternative explanation for an item of evolution evidence, students worked in small groups to brainstorm. In most cases, it is not difficult to conjure up an alternative explanation as credible or more credible than the evolution explanation. One major difficulty was to provide a non-evolutionary explanation as to why fossils are strung out simple to complex in the geological column. This formula, which was published in a science periodical, occurred to me:

habitat + population size + size and structure
= Relative Fossil Production Potential (RFPP)

This means that a clam, for example, is ideal for fossil production, while a terrestrial animal like a horse is not. Fossils are strung out, not in the order in which they evolved into existence, but on the basis of RFPP. Simple organisms have a much greater likelihood of producing fossils than large, complex organisms. In deep rock strata where it is most difficult to discover fossils, one will most likely find fossils of simple organisms with a high RFPP and no fossils of large complex organisms with a low RFPP. In addition, the RFPP explanation for the stringing-out predicts that no intermediate fossils, which would indicate evolution had occurred, will be found. Given what we know about the fossilization process, one would think that any explanation for the fossil record would have to take RFPP into consideration, but that would make the evolution explanation superfluous. RFPP, the counterinductive explanation, is the ordinary, everyday explanation for the stringing out of fossils from simple to complex, while the evolution explanation is the extraordinary explanation.

I was so convinced that the textbook evolution format was a fraudulent methodology that I submitted an Evolution Curriculum Revision Proposal to several committees, composed exclusively of educators and the board of education, all of whom roundly rejected it. Their unreasonable defense was to claim that to even question evolution is akin to teaching creation. Thus, they were defending evolution from criticism by keeping counterinduction out, but at the same time, they were formatting the curriculum to represent doctrine rather than theory. The incongruity seemed lost on them: the only way evolution can be taught in a science classroom is to allow criticism; otherwise, the scientific integrity of the classroom is violated. Actually, creation is directly mentioned in reference to only one aspect of evolution evidence and that is comparative anatomy. Why do similarities exist among organisms? The Religious Humanist, which was Darwin's religious orientation, will claim that similarities exist because organisms evolved from a common ancestor. The creationist, on the other hand, will claim that similarities exist because organisms were created with similarities. Neither explanation is testable. By the way, Religious Humanism, an atheistic religion, was ruled a bona fide religion by the U.S. Supreme Court. This was Darwin's religious orientation and quite likely the driving force behind his data interpretations:

> A man who has no assured and no present belief in the existence of a personal God or a future existence with retribution and rewards, can have for his rule of life, as far as I can see, only to follow those impulses and instincts which are the strongest or which seem to him the best ones. A dog acts in this manner, but he does so blindly. A man on the other hand, looks forwards and backwards, and compares his various feelings, desires, and recollections. He then finds, in accordance with the verdict of the wisest men, that the highest satisfaction is derived from following certain impulses, namely the social instincts.[69]

Darwin's evolution belief could easily serve as a doctrine for Religious Humanism, just as creation serves as a doctrine for Christianity:

> Religious humanists regard the universe as self-existing and not created. Humanism believes that man is part of nature and that he emerged as the result of a continuous process. We find insufficient evidence for the belief in the existence of a supernatural; it is either meaningless or irrelevant to the question of survival and fulfillment of the human race. As nontheists we begin with humans not God, nature not deity.[70]

No other biology teacher from either of two high schools was willing to participate in petitioning for an evolution curriculum revision reform. Out of curiosity I wrote a paper entitled *On Being Considerate of Traditions,* which I delivered to each of the eight or nine science teachers in the high school where I taught and asked for a response. The paper addressed the issue of discrimination toward creationist students in the classroom and scientific methodology, among other things. I shortly received a written response from the science department chairman, the gist of which stated that the science teachers did not intend to respond. I thought he had been appointed to speak for all the science teachers and that was the end of the matter. But a month later I received a response from several science teachers who had gotten together. The pertinent statement in their response is this one relative to the evolution curriculum: "If a theory or point of view is treated only as a doctrine to be validated, and not one to be challenged, it is not within the realm of science." That precisely states my reason for submitting the evolution curriculum reform proposal. No science teacher, or scientist, for that matter, can dispute that assessment. So why would they not support the proposal when it was submitted? They were too intimidated. They did not want to incur the wrath of the local institution hierarchies that had revealed themselves to be opposed to the proposal, not to mention committed evolutionists on the staff. It is quite likely that evolution dogmatism is taught under duress by many teachers in many school districts who would much prefer to challenge evolution the way it is meant to be challenged in a science classroom.

It is really an incredible situation when one stops to think about it. Counterinductive thinking is universally applied in all investigations.

What other way can one discover the whys and wherefores about some event or phenomenon? Evolution research is probably the one and only exception to the rule. It is the product of research in which counterinduction is deliberately and rabidly banned. In criminal investigations, for example, one can say that counterinduction is the accused person's defense. Meanwhile, the subliminal message to the deceived creationist students is that they are guilty of believing in an explanation for origins that cannot be scientifically sustained as can evolution. Therefore, evolution, it is implied, has the endorsement of science, a much-admired and trusted institution, and because of that endorsement, there is no need to question the evidence. But science based upon authoritarianism went out with the Middle Ages. In a modern science classroom, as in a courtroom, the evidence is counterinductively questioned, and that is the creationist student's defense, as well as proper procedure.

Origins Research Is Metaphysical, Not Practical

Darwin was able to play fast and loose with scientific methodology because origins research is metaphysical, meaning no compelling practicality exists that would dictate how the evidence must be interpreted. On the other hand, everyday, real-time research is amenable to experimentation and has some kind of practical reward, such as a monetary or labor-saving reward to offer. That practicality dictates how evidence will be interpreted and religion is not a factor, as is the case with evolution. Evolution has no practical application in our lives; it exists entirely for religious reasons. It is religious bias and not a compelling practicality that dictates how the evolution evidence will be interpreted, and Darwin took full advantage of that fact. The following two quotes regarding intelligent design exemplify the metaphysical quality of origins research:

> To suppose that the eye with all its inimitable contrivances for adjusting the focus to different amounts of light, and for the correction of spherical and chromatic aberration, could have been formed by natural selection, seems, I freely confess, absurd in the highest degree.[71]

It is logical to assume that intelligent designs require an intelligent designer. The same assessment can most likely be said for every kind of organ in every organism. According to the quote, Darwin is ultimately questioning his faith in the nonexistence of God, but establishing a belief in the nonexistence of God is the religious imperative that drives evolution. There is only one way out of the dilemma and that is to defy logic and boldly declare a belief that natural selection, a mindless, random process, can create intelligent designs, an incongruity that requires a rather large leap of faith. But the religious imperative is more important than facts and logic:

> I entirely reject, as in my judgment quite unnecessary, any subsequent addition "of new powers and attributes and forces"; or of any "principles of improvement," except insofar as every character which is naturally selected or preserved is in some way an advantage or improvement, otherwise it would not have been selected. If I were convinced that I required such additions to the theory of natural selection, I would reject it as rubbish. . . . I would give nothing for the theory of natural selection if it requires miraculous additions at any one stage of descent.[72]

In the first quote logic prevails, but in the second quote religion prevails and there is no compelling practicality to dictate otherwise. The precedent is that, if Darwin can waver between two opposing explanations for an earth's origins evidence, why are students not granted the same privilege, which would allow them to interpret the evolution evidence in other ways that would suit their religious preferences?

Present-day evolution proponents have chosen a different tactic. Rather than defy logic and insist that evolution can create intelligent designs, they are trying to use the courts to outlaw consideration of intelligent design from the evolution curriculum altogether. If that is not brazen thought control, nothing is. Extreme measures have to be taken by evolution dogmatists to censor intelligent design because it directly contradicts evolution's religious imperative to "ungod the universe."[73]

Jevons's Elementary Rule of Logic

Was Darwin correct in abandoning natural selection or can one simply ignore the incipiency problem, as the science establishment has done for well over 100 years? This is a rare case when a conclusion — Darwin's conclusion that natural selection is incompetent — makes a prediction that can validate or invalidate the conclusion. The prediction is this: if natural selection had been functioning in the past, one should find forensic evidence in the form of numerous transitional fossils in the earth's crust. The prediction is not fulfilled:

> The extreme rarity of transitional forms in the fossil record persists as the trade secret of paleontology. The evolutionary trees that adorn our textbooks have data only at the tips and nodes of their branches; the rest is inference, however reasonable, not the evidence of fossils. Yet Darwin was so wedded to gradualism that he wagered his entire theory on a denial of this literal record.[74]

Now we discover that we are teaching students an explanation for origins that fails Jevons's elementary rule of logic: "A single absolute conflict between fact and hypothesis is fatal to the hypothesis; *falsa in uno falsa in omnibus.*" W. Stanley Jevons, in his book *The Principles of Science — A Treatise on Logic and the Scientific Method,* is simply stating the obvious because his rule of logic is everybody's rule of logic. It is a rule that everybody, consciously or subconsciously, follows in their daily lives of decision-making.

Strangely, Darwin did make reference to what we know today as Jevons's rule of logic when he made this concession:

> The geological record is extremely imperfect and this fact will to a large extent explain why we do not find interminable varieties, connecting together all the extinct and existing forms of life by the finest graduated steps. He who rejects these views on the nature of the geological record, will rightly reject my whole theory.[75]

Creation predicts that no irrefutable transitional fossil will be discovered. Darwin withheld that information, as do present-day textbook authors. Personally, Darwin could not bring himself to abide by Jevons's rule of logic, thus his ad hoc excuse that intermediates would some day be discovered. Amazingly, Darwin and the evolution establishment have perpetuated an explanation for origins that from the very outset has defied an elementary rule of logic. That indicates how much religious evangelism rules the thinking of evolution proponents. Every explanation for origins has a religious imperative behind it. The religious imperative behind evolution apparently is to coerce the belief in God out of the collective consciousness of society.

Natural selection is vulnerable in other ways. For example, Darwin used imaginary examples of natural selection rather than valid observed examples. What is more, the only example of natural selection in the *Origin* that dealt with the origin of a species is how Darwin imagined bears could become whale-like animals. That example was in the first edition but removed from the five subsequent editions. It was probably thought to strain the credulity of the reader too much, and the *Origin* is indeed a book of persuasion, not proof.

Because Darwin could not report having observed natural selection, he made it analogous to the artificial selection of domestic animals by man. But in doing so he inadvertently set the stage for an analysis fatal to natural selection: the two names tell us that natural selection and artificial selection cannot be analogous, as Darwin mistakenly postulated, but the antithesis of one another. Man is an intelligent, persistent, and consistent selector, which means, according to Darwin's analogy, persistent and consistent selectors exist in nature. Students seem to enjoy considering the various examples of natural selection that one finds in the *Origin* and in the textbooks, identifying the selectors, and determining that they cannot possibly be persistent and consistent selectors because they cannot control the reproductive environment as man does. One cannot analyze natural selection in terms of a vague generalization; instead, one must think in terms of identifiable selectors. By the way, the selectors that were supposed to change bears into whale-like animals were insects swimming in the water. Evolution is the ideal subject for teaching students critical thinking, while revealing the lack of it in the curriculum. Darwin was trying to prove the impossible — that a random, mindless mechanism can create intelligent designs. Today, textbook authors are trying to do the same thing; it is no wonder the curriculum so often defies logic.

Critique of an Evolution Unit

The *Modern Biology*[76] textbook has been on the market for many years; in fact, I have a facsimile of the 1921 edition, which, at that time, was entitled *Biology for Beginners*. The textbook overall has a well-organized format. The evolution unit itself is on a par with other evolution units in other textbooks that I have reviewed. I do not mean to single out the evolution unit in *Modern Biology* as being any better or worse than that in other textbooks. One thing all the textbooks avoid is non-evolutionary counterinductive thinking in their presentation of the evolution evidence. Counterinductive thinking is critical thinking.

I noted that the authors had to resort to an imaginary example of natural selection when introducing the alleged mechanism. That in itself speaks volumes. Natural selection is laid out like this in the typical biology textbook: variations exist; no two members of a species are exactly alike. There is a tendency for populations to overproduce and outstrip their food supply, but that rarely happens. The crucial question is, what is holding populations in check? The evolutionists' imaginary answer is that natural selection is keeping populations in check by removing the less fit, which results in the evolution of some of the population into a new species. Natural selection's incipiency problem is censored from the curriculum.

The evolutionists' answer to what is holding populations in check is extraordinary and mythical. The real answer to what is holding populations in check is an ordinary random natural selection, having nothing to do with an alleged evolution process. Random natural selection is observed and not a myth. Several examples of random natural selection could be mentioned, but consider just one, the wolf and caribou relationship, which was observed. Wolves do not test the herd in order to find the slightly slower healthy caribou, whose slow genes would then supposedly be eliminated, while also supposedly eliminating slow genes among the wolves; instead they test the herd to find the caribou made slow and diseased by old age. There is nothing evolutionary about that. It is unlikely that slow genes in wolves would be eliminated because the pack shares the kill. Seed dispersal is random and the circumstances that place a prey and predator in proximity to one another are random. Random natural selection is taken for granted. In all of recorded history, to my knowledge, no other kind of selection has been observed that would remotely suggest macroevolution.

The *Modern Biology* authors discuss mutations, the occurrence of which is a vital necessity for evolution. According to the evolution scenario, mutations would have to occur by the countless billions. When I began teaching, textbook authors would discuss mutations by pointing out, for example, albinism in plants and animals, hornless cattle, and seedless fruit. The authors were making the point that mutations do occur. It does nothing for the credibility of evolution to point out that harmful-for-survival mutations occur, unless one is determined to take advantage of students' youthful trust and ignorance. I would make the point with students that evolution requires useful-for-survival mutations, not harmful-for-survival mutations that are actually a reduction in traits. Today, according to the 2006 *Modern Biology* textbook, authors no longer try to deceive students with harmful-for-survival mutations. In fact, the only mutation actually discussed is about bacteria becoming resistant to antibiotics, which does not fill the bill. First, it is an example of artificial selection, not natural selection; man is doing the selecting. Second, we do not know if a mutation actually occurred making the bacteria resistant to the antibiotic or if the gene for resistance was already in the gene pool, meaning the antibiotic could never have been 100 percent lethal. That is an example of counterinductive thinking defending objective science against dogmatism or, to use another term, authoritarianism.

Under the heading of MUTATIONS, the following sentences are expressed: "Many mutations are harmful, although some have no effect. Because natural selection operates only on genes that are expressed, it is very slow to eliminate harmful recessive mutations. In the long run, however, beneficial mutations are a vital part of evolution." Such as? No examples of beneficial mutations are provided. It is not possible to prove a negative, that useful-for-survival mutations do not occur, but the burden of proof, that useful-for-survival mutations do occur, is on the evolutionists' shoulders. Without unequivocal observational reports of useful-for-survival mutations, Jevons's rule of logic becomes applicable. Interestingly, the fossil record, which, from my experience, was always a central feature in the evolution unit, has been demoted to the glossary. Is it because there is a growing awareness among the lay public that the fossil record is devoid of transitional fossils, in which case, Jevons's rule of logic becomes applicable? Evolution predicts the existence of useful-for-survival mutations and transitional fossils.

The authors discuss Hardy-Weinberg genetic equilibrium: if five assumptions occur in a population, evolution will not occur. The five assumptions are: no net mutations occur, individuals either enter or leave the population, the population is large, individuals mate randomly, and selection does not occur. Students are likely to read those five assumptions and conclude that if any one or more of them are not fulfilled, evolution will inevitably occur. It is a backhanded way of proving evolution will occur with a scenario that proves how evolution will not occur. It is based upon a preconceived belief in evolution on the part of Hardy and Weinberg. But does evolution really occur if any one or more of those assumptions are not fulfilled? Young students are not sophisticated enough to ask that question, but it should occur to the teacher. The last assumption, if selection does not occur, seems to be redundant. What is selection but another word for evolution in action? So what the assumption is saying is, if evolution does not occur, evolution will not occur.

The important issue of transitional fossils is given short shrift. Four skeletal drawings are provided of the pakicetus, ambulocetus, dorudon, and the whale. The first two are terrestrial animals and all three are touted as the evolutionary ancestors of the whale. That is the extraordinary scenario, but the ordinary scenario is that the first three are simply extinct species and have nothing to do with evolution. The authors are following Darwin's lead and censoring alternative points of view. One can make comparisons down to the molecular level, but comparisons will never prove evolution unless one is predisposed to believe they do. The authors are also omitting a very important detail. The pakicetus and the ambulocetus, which were terrestrial, presumably gave birth to their offspring head first in order to avoid suffocation during birthing. Whales give birth to their offspring tail first, presumably to avoid drowning during birthing. Try inventing a credible evolution scenario that will account for that birthing switch.

The evolution unit relies heavily on drawings and photographs to show variations within species populations, such as facial features in monkeys and coloration, body size, and tongue lengths in various animals. Only a true believer can extrapolate those cosmetic features into evidence for macroevolution. Does anyone believe that all individuals in a species must be unequivocally alike in every detail? If the skeptic does not, if variety is to be expected, then minor variations within a species population mean nothing in terms of evolution.

The evolution unit discusses coevolution, which allegedly is when two or more species have evolved adaptations to each other's influence.

One example is the pollination of flowers by insects. The authors do not go into it, but imagine the questions students might ask if they were encouraged to do so. Exactly how is the insect supposed to influence the flower and vice versa? How can the flower anticipate what adaptation will serve the insect and vice versa? The adaptations would begin as useless incipient cell structures. How would the flower and the insect survive that uselessness? What causes the incipient adaptations to become useful simultaneously? It would be tragic if the insect evolved a proboscis, while the flower had not yet developed the capability to produce nectar or vice versa. It is as though a strategy exists whereby simply giving a scientific name to a difficulty, coevolution, will actually dispel the difficulty, and perhaps it does in the minds of uncritical thinkers.

The textbook has a section entitled "Evolution in Action." So far, the unit has been smoke and mirrors, but now we apparently are getting down to some hard evidence. The anole lizards on some islands in the Caribbean have distinct body types. Some lizards frequent the ground and tree trunks, some live on the branches, and still others live in tall grass. Several species of twig-dwelling lizards exist on various islands, yet they are distinctly different. How did that happen? It could be that several ancestral species specialized for living on twigs originally lived on one island and later migrated to other islands. The authors do not inform the reader whether or not the species on the various islands are actually distinct species and cannot interbreed. Migration is the ordinary explanation. According to the authors, DNA suggests that the lizards did not migrate, but evolved independently and happened to evolve similar adaptations, which the authors refer to as convergent evolution. That is the extraordinary explanation. At any rate, the heading of that section of the book is highly misleading; no evolution in action was observed. The alleged co-evolution between flowers and insect was also discussed under that same heading. Apparently, whatever the authors speculate about what occurred in the past is the same as real-time action. In their zeal to promote an evolution belief, the authors are taking advantage of students' youthful trust and gullibility.

I have at hand four editions of *Modern Biology*. The 1921 edition does not have a chapter on alleged human evolution, nor does the 1956 edition. In fact, the chapter on evolution in that book is entitled "The Changing World of Life." The word "evolution" cannot be found in the entire book. The 1993 edition does have a chapter on alleged human evolution, but the 2006 edition does not.

After Sputnik was launched by the Russians, there was panic in some quarter that the United States was falling behind the Russians in science and technology. The federal government got into the textbook-writing business, which was written by committees. It was overkill. We had three choices for biology textbooks: the blue version (molecular), the green version (ecological), and the yellow version (general). We used the yellow version for quite a few years. It was probably true of all textbook publishers at the time that evolution was suddenly given considerable emphasis. The authors did not hesitate to propagandize evolution throughout the book at the slightest opportunity, and human evolution speculation was rampant. When I taught that topic, I had several different biology books on hand. I would remind students that an artist's rendition of what a skull looked like with flesh on it is not an exact science. To make the point, I had one book with a skull, *Pithecanthropus erectus,* that could pass for a man on the street, while in another book it was made to look like the first cousin to an ape. We do not know if the skulls have anything to do with evolution or not.

The evolution unit consists of wishful thinking scenarios, hypothetical charts, hypothetical graphs, photographs, and drawings showing variety within a species. In other words, a host of nebulous information exists just begging to be critically analyzed. By the way, the authors define microevolution as "a change in the collective genetic material of a population," but the word "macroevolution" is not in the book. I would define macroevolution as the origin of a new species, by means of natural selection, which is capable of living in a different niche in the ecosystem and able to mate only within its own species. It is a gross error on the part of the authors not to clearly delineate what it is they are trying to prove or persuade the students to believe.

I recall several items of information in the evolution unit that have come and gone; at least they are not in the 2006 *Modern Biology* textbook. These include the *coelacanth*, a primitive-looking fish; the Piltdown man, discovered to be a hoax; alleged ancestral fossils of the horse; the *archaeopteryx*; a fossil imprint of a feathered bird; a chapter on alleged human evolution; and selection of the peppered moths. Artificial selection is briefly presented, not as a substitute for natural selection, as Darwin presented it, but only to show that variety exists in domestic plants and animals. The fossil record has become a liability, probably because it fails to show transitional fossils. I predict that the alleged ancestral fossils of the whale will be removed from the textbooks. The removal of these items of information occurred for various reasons, not the least of which is critical thinking. The evolution unit is gradually revealing itself to be less substantive and more and more superficial, to the point of being composed primarily of the single-minded, wishful thinking of the authors.

A survey indicates no item of evidence uniquely supports evolution and evolution only, which means alternative points of view exist. The authors failed to provide alternative explanations for the untestable/circumstantial evidence typically found in the textbooks, such as comparative anatomy, geographic distribution, comparative embryology, and vestigial parts. All investigations, except evolution, give alternative points of view adequate consideration, as common sense or common intelligence dictates. Science has been described as codified common sense. But, when evolution is taught, students are required to suspend their own innate common sense as well as that of legitimate science and surrender to Darwinian dogmatism. Students do not question the evolution data because they are not told it is questionable. From a learner outcome perspective, that constitutes a kind of scholastic abuse for the purpose of indoctrination. Advocates of evolution should temper their advocacy with an awareness that they quite likely have been taught only half of the subject and that another world of counterinductive information has been withheld from them.

The typical secondary school evolution curriculum is a perfect example of authoritarianism, a pseudoscience that came and went in the Middle Ages. The authenticity for an explanation for a phenomenon is ultimately determined, not on the evidence so much as on the basis of the prestige and professional reputation of the investigator. Authoritarianism is just the opposite of objective science. Counterinduction, an integral part of objective science, is deemed not necessary because the authoritarian has spoken and that is all that is required. Thus, when the story of evolution is told to students, they are conditioned to accept it without question, just the way the authoritarian authors present it. What is more, the story of evolution is based upon mythical evidence. Real science, unlike authoritarianism, does not take an investigator's word that critical items of evidence exist. For example, natural selection, transitional fossils, and useful-for-survival mutations represent essential, yet mythical, evidence.

This is the way real science deals with those items of mythical evidence. Evolving organs would have to begin as incipient, useless structures, and because they are a non-functioning conglomeration of matter, they provide no selection advantage. In other words, the alleged natural selection mechanism is pointless, which explains why it is not observed. The slogan "survival of the fittest," which provides credence to the idea of natural selection, is also a myth. What we observe in nature are members of species that exist and can reproduce. They require no greater level of fitness than that. In other words, by those standards, all the individuals of a species are equally fit. What if a few members of a population can move a little faster than average or have a slightly different coloration? Even the most vivid imagination cannot extrapolate those cosmetic features into the beginning of a new species. It is random natural selection, not evolutionary natural selection, that is observed in the ecosystem.

Because evolutionary natural selection is a myth, it follows that transitional fossils are a myth. And because evolutionary natural selection and transitional fossils are a myth, it follows that useful-for-survival mutations are a myth. Useful-for-survival mutations apparently occur only in the minds of evolutionists. The incipiency problem is censored because it is the key that exposes the entire mythology.

The ultimate source of the pervasive authoritarianism in the evolution curriculum is religion. Objective science is rejected because it cannot validate an atheistic world view that is central to Religious Humanism. Religious Humanism needs science as the medium for promoting an atheistic world view, but only a subverted brand of science will do the indoctrination job for them. Teachers are expected to do all the deceptive teaching, not because science requires it, but because evolution's religious imperative requires it. I refused to do it. All in all, the evolution unit indicates, as Asa Gray would say, "a bias which, to say the least of it, is very far from becoming in a lover of science."[77]

This is my advice to prospective students. The evolution evidence exists in a category that has alternative explanations as credible, or more credible, than the evolution explanations. Do not be mentally passive; think counterinductively. Most likely the evolution unit will censor intelligent design and natural selection's incipiency problem. They are legitimate items of knowledge within the body of knowledge about evolution. Help end the censorship and make those items of discussion common knowledge. The evolution unit will report evolution evidences as though they unequivocally exist, such as useful-for-survival mutations, transitional fossils, and observations of evolutionary natural selection. Do not accept substitutes and half measures. Do not be gullible; be skeptical, that is the correct scientific attitude. In other words, defend objective science against authoritarianism. The real tragedy is not that students have to be alerted to an indoctrinating evolution curriculum, but that the indoctrinating curriculum even exists.

Applied Creation

I employed the concept of applied creation whenever I taught the evolution curriculum. Applied creation is not a separate curriculum with its own set of data. Instead it is a concept kept in mind and tied to the evolution data; a sounding board, if you will. To be honest, a teacher should inform students at the outset that every item of evolution evidence has an alternative explanation to consider. Applied creation is not unconstitutional, but creation science was ruled unconstitutional because it is tailored to enhance the credibility of a particular belief system. That ruling should, in all fairness, also apply to evolution authoritarianism because it is undeniably tailored and serves as a doctrine for some belief systems as well.

Applied creation is a teaching tool that serves to bring critical thinking into the evolution curriculum. Without an alternative explanation for origins to bear in mind, it is difficult to even contemplate the reality of evolution dogmatism, especially when it emanates from an institution that is otherwise noted as a paragon of honesty and objectivity. Applied creation eliminates evolution dogmatism, makes the evolution methodology scientifically acceptable, makes the curriculum constitutionally legal and educationally ethical, eliminates discrimination, and foils evolution's religious imperative to "ungod the universe."[78]

Educators often discuss subject matter in terms of learner outcomes. The dogmatic evolution curriculum attempts to instill a disbelief in God as its primary learner outcome. The applied creation curriculum defends a belief in God as its primary learner outcome, but within the context of the evolution data. Thus, two curriculums are available, based essentially on identical evolution data, but with completely opposite learner outcomes. Parents and students should have the right to choose the learner outcome they desire when the evolution data are taught.

The Earth's Origins Evidence Is Public Domain

The earth's origins evidence is, by natural law, public domain by virtue of the fact we all reside equally on the planet and can make no special claims on the origins evidence. So when Darwin determined to interpret the earth's origins evidence exclusively to fit his personal belief system, he was confiscating public property. This could not have been done had a segment of the science establishment not aided and abetted.

The time is long past due when the earth's origins evidence is wrested from the evolution dogmatists and returned to the public. Legitimate scientific methodology, educational idealism, and a compassionate consideration of alternative beliefs all stand opposed to a curriculum that is unconstitutional, unscientific, indoctrinating, and discriminatory. The United States Supreme Court, in *Edwards v. Aguilard*, has ruled against creation science because it represented a tailored curriculum, tailored to enhance a belief in creation. Other U.S. Supreme Court decisions have ruled against curriculums that are close-minded for the purpose of enhancing the credibility of points of view. No one gave evolution dogmatists a special dispensation to ignore U.S. Supreme Court decisions while other beliefs about origins must bow to them. The U.S. Constitution and legitimate science are as one in opposition to Darwinian dogmatism. And why not? It requires a high degree of religious fanaticism to promote a dogmatic evolution curriculum aimed at deceiving a nation's youth.

Given the metaphysical nature of origins research, science cannot empirically prove any explanation for origins that would cause it to be universally and unequivocally accepted. Should evidence present itself that is contrary to one's belief about origins, one may simply ignore the evidence, as evolutionists do regarding intelligent design. Presently, evolution is in the curriculum, not as being proved or as having the remotest possibility of being proved, but to denigrate other beliefs about origins. It is not the purpose of a science classroom to be socially divisive, and parents and students who do not like it should not put up with it. Nor is it the purpose of a science classroom or any other public school classroom to indoctrinate rather than educate students regarding a subject.

Biology is defined as the study of living things. The metaphysical nature of origins research precludes the possibility of biology dealing with the origin of living things in a decisive way. The study of living things and the origin of living things are two separate dimensions that biology is unable to encompass. The question of the origin of living things should be relegated to religion, philosophy, or to a science establishment that candidly admits its limitations.

Fundamental Concepts Reviewed

The *Origin of Species* was originally written for adults who can presumably fend for themselves as to the way the book is formatted and how persuasive the contents are to them. But the book took on an entirely new dimension when the essence of it was integrated into biology and subsequently taught in science classrooms. The moment that occurred, Darwin's dogmatism became an unacceptable imitation of true science and a violation of academic freedom. Meanwhile, without adults to protect them by pointing out Darwin's shortcomings as a researcher, students became victims of a great deception. Students have an inalienable right to have a scientifically objective evolution curriculum taught, in keeping with the standards and procedures common to other scientific investigation.

Parents who do not want their sons or daughters exposed to evolution's atheistic religious imperative have a right, which is grounded in true science, the U.S. Constitution, and educational idealism, to remove their child from the curriculum or insist that a scientifically objective evolution curriculum be taught.

There is no such thing as a secular explanation for origins, as evolution proponents would have us believe. All explanations for origins are inherently and unavoidably religious and, therefore, have religious imperatives behind them. Because explanations for origins evidence lack a compelling practicality and are instead guided by metaphysical considerations, they will not be universally accepted. There will always be dissenters. The dissenters become victims of discrimination when their points of view are not tolerated. Evolution cannot be conclusively proved because that would require witnessing and recording macroevolution in real time, over long ages. The question of origins is beyond the capabilities of the science endeavor. One can only speculate about the meaning of the earth's origins evidence and that means, in terms of scientific objectivity, speculating from every conceivable point of view by the science establishment or anyone else so inclined. But scientific objectivity becomes heresy when it contradicts a religious imperative, hidden or not hidden behind a particular explanation.

It becomes apparent that evolution is a failed explanation for origins when counterinduction is allowed. That does not mean that some other explanation is proved and must be universally accepted. The fact that evolution cannot hold its own when counterinduction is allowed, as Darwin well knew, is today conceivably well known among select circles in the upper echelons of science, education, and religion. If that is so, the various hierarchies will not own up to something that is a scandalous betrayal of students' trust. Besides, they have a great advantage going — they are able to use tax supported public schools to promote a materialistic belief in origins under the banner of theory, which is really doctrine in disguise. Students' academic freedom is denied whenever evolution dogmatism is taught to them under the pretense of theory. In my mind, as a student advocate, that calculated denial of academic freedom extends beyond ethics to criminal intent. A great nation is grounded in great institutions, but institutions that conspire to deceive a nation's youth end up diminishing the greatness of that nation.

Conclusion

This is the valid conclusion one comes to when a scientifically objective evolution curriculum is taught: one cannot determine with scientific certainty how a multitude of organisms came into existence on planet Earth, but the evidence indicates it did not occur by means of an alleged evolution process. That being the case, it is no wonder evolutionists do not practice scientific objectivity. If a credible materialistic explanation for origins exists, it has not yet been discovered.

One is free to believe what one wants about origins, but students should not believe that evolution is a product of objective science.

Actually, students are not allowed to be free thinkers because they are in a mandatory setting, while being covertly taught a misrepresentation of real science. Evolution is really a product of Darwin's brand of pseudoscientific authoritarianism, which, as I have amply revealed, systematically selects and rejects evidence according to a preconceived belief in evolution. The creation versus evolution debate is basically a debate within the domain of science between two methodologies, namely, objective science and authoritarianism.

Evolution has its own brand of authoritarianism because it is uniquely dedicated to answering the question of origins. Evolution's methodology is limited to naturalism, not because science requires it, but because the religious imperative requires it. A true explanation for a phenomenon may exist, but if it is outside the boundary of naturalism the investigator cannot go there. For example, intelligent design cannot be addressed because it is outside the naturalism boundary. It is a way to justify and dignify bias. The investigator cannot be blamed because he is merely following the dictates of a naturalism methodology. Science itself does not require an exclusive naturalism methodology. The methodology has nothing to do with science but is rooted in evolution's religious imperative to promote an atheistic explanation for origins. When Darwin determined not to consider alternative points of view, it was supernatural points of view that he apparently had in mind. Real science has no boundaries that might cater to an investigator's biases. The earth's origin evidence is public domain, and no compelling practicality exists that gives precedence to one explanation over others. No one has the authority to impose a methodology on students that would dictate which items of evidence will or will not be considered and how evidence will or will not be interpreted.

In the debate between competing methodologies, one item of earth's origins evidence, intelligent design, comes to the forefront. Everyone can observe intelligent design in nature, and that is a powerful indicator as to the existence of a Supreme Being. Evolution dogmatists agree. Otherwise, they would not be taking steps to prevent America's youth from considering intelligent design in the evolution curriculum. That action constitutes an admission to a conflicting fact, which in turn terminates the debate, according to Jevons's rule of logic. That is the obvious conclusion of objective science; however, if one's belief in evolution is so compelling that it overrides conflicting facts, then evolution remains viable and authoritarianism rules.

It is apparent that all explanations for origins are inherently and unavoidably religious and, therefore, destined to be susceptible to tailoring. It is also apparent, given the metaphysical status of origins research, that it is unlikely that science can unequivocally prove any explanation for origins that would cause it to be universally acceptable. Consequently, speaking from experience, a teacher who attempts to preserve the scientific integrity of the classroom by subjecting evolution data to alternative points of view has a considerable likelihood of finding himself working in a very hostile environment, courtesy of the proponents of the data that are supposed to be questioned. The evolutionists' strategy is to portray evolution as theoretical, yet somehow unquestionable, which is an irreconcilable contradiction. Evolutionists do not want students to realize that evolution is religiously doctrinal and, therefore, a sacrilege to question the data. What evolutionists want students to believe is that evolution is factual to the point of being beyond question. How is this false factuality established? By thought control, by following Darwin's lead and ignoring alternative points of view at the outset, and by conditioning students into becoming subservient automatons without a notion that the evolution observations are open to alternative points of view.

Two solutions to the origins curriculum dilemma come to mind, one of which is to include all explanations for origins and question all of the data. Why not? All explanations for origins are fantastically out of the ordinary, including evolution. Darwin's grand strategy, in keeping with his religious imperative, was to formulate a mundane, naturalistic explanation for origins that is ongoing in the ecosystem and did not defer to the supernatural. But that meant evolution would be relentlessly subject to critical observation. If the creative mechanism, natural selection, is ordinary and ongoing, then the mechanism itself and everything about it should be observable. Darwin could not confirm natural selection with actual observations, which is why he tried to make artificial selection serve as the observable substitute. From a science perspective, natural selection is not real but a phantom mechanism, a supernatural mechanism existing only in the minds of believers. And, if natural selection is a phantom mechanism, then it is predictable that useful-for-survival mutations and intermediate fossils are figments of imagination as well. All of this means that evolution is no more qualified for a place in the science textbooks than other explanations for origins that avowedly defer to the supernatural.

The second solution is to remove the question of origins from the biology curriculum altogether. That is not as farfetched as it may seem. A look at the evolution unit in a typical textbook reveals that it is replete with unsubstantiated wishful thinking on the part of the authors, but devoid of counterinductive thinking. That format disqualifies it as legitimate science.

At any rate, the present evolution curriculum format poses questions pertinent to legislators, theologians, scientists, educators, court justices, and last but not least, parents of the victims of an indoctrinating curriculum. Why is evolution, a doctrine of Religious Humanism, in the biology curriculum in public schools all by its unquestionable, unscientific self? Does that not violate the popular concept of objective science? Is that not also a violation of a Constitution dedicated to religious freedom and the separation of church and state? Yet putting aside religious preferences, it is fundamentally a morally right or wrong issue. It is patently wrong to take advantage of youthful ignorance and teach an evolution curriculum that misrepresents true science. All of the above-mentioned professions have a vested interest in an origins curriculum; hopefully, one or more of them will take the initiative to correct that wrong.

It does not matter who protests and from what perspective they protest, nor is it of any consequence that the science establishment has lowered its standards to accommodate evolution. The science teacher has only one choice and that is to teach a scientifically objective evolution curriculum; anything less is science fiction. Besides, a scientifically objective evolution curriculum is the only methodology teachers can teach that will not unconstitutionally tailor the curriculum. The true science teacher must defend objective science against evolutionists' religion-dominated, antiquated authoritarianism. Science teachers are hired to teach only one brand of science that will preserve the scientific integrity of the classroom and that is objective science. The dedicated science teacher, following professional standards, resists dictating interpretations of the earth's origins evidence, while opening the evidence up to alternative points of view. That curriculum strategy should have the support of the entire science establishment.

Endnotes

1. N. Barlow, *The Autobiography of Charles Darwin* (New York: Harcourt, Brace and Co., 1958), p. 115.

2. H. Ward, *Charles Darwin: The Man and His Warfare* (Indianapolis, IN: The Bobbs-Merrill Co., 1927), p. 288.

3. Ibid., p. 296.

4. A. Gray, *Darwiniana* (Cambridge, MA: Harvard University Press, 1963, reprint of the 1876 edition), p. 110.

5. C. Bibby, *Scientists Extraordinary* (New York: Pergamon Press, 1972), p. 6.

6. Ward, *Charles Darwin: The Man and His Warfare*, p. 246.

7. P. Appleman, *Darwin* (New York: W.W. Norton Co., Inc., 1970), p. 632–633.

8. Ibid., p. 633.

9. R. Hedtke, "The Episteme Is the Theory," *Creation Research Society Quarterly*, vol.18, no.1 (June 1981); p 9–10.

10. Ibid, p. 78.

11. C. Darwin, *On the Origin of Species*, first edition.

12. M. Peckham, *The Origin of Species: A Variorum Text* (Philadelphia, PA: University of Pennsylvania Press, 1959), p. 333–334.

13. Ibid., p. 9.

14. Ibid., p. 9.

15. S. Butler, *Evolution, Old and New* (Boston, MA: S.E. Cassino Publ., 1879), p. 359.

16. G. Himmelfarb, *Darwin and the Darwinian Revolution* (London: Chatto and Windus, 1959), p. 244–245.

17. Ibid., p. 287–288.

18. Ibid., p. 261–288.

19. Barlow, *The Autobiography of Charles Darwin*, p. 123.

20. C. Darwin, *On the Origin of Species* (New York: The Modern Library, 1872), p. 168.

21. Ibid., p. 178.

22. Himmelfarb, *Darwin and the Darwinian Revolution*, p. 273–274.

23. F. Darwin, *Foundations of the Origin of Species* (Cambridge, UK; New York: Cambridge University Press, 1909), p. 109.

24. J. Merchant, *Russell Wallace: Letters and Reminiscences* (Cambridge, UK; New York: Cambridge University Press, 1916), p. 142–143.

25. D. Hull, *Darwin and His Critics* (Cambridge, MA: Harvard University Press, 1973), p. 270.

26. C. Darlington, "The Origin of Darwinism," *Scientific American* 1959, 200(5): 60–66.

27. Ibid.

28. R. Colp, *To Be an Invalid* (Chicago, IL: University of Chicago Press, 1977), p. 142.

29. G. Pickering, *Creative Malady* (Oxford: Oxford University Press, 1974), p. 71.

30. Ibid., p. 32–33.

31. Ibid., p. 74.

32. Colp, *To Be an Invalid*, p. 143.

33. Pickering, *Creative Malady*, p. 75.

34. Ibid., p. 91.

35. Colp, *To Be an Invalid*, p. xiii.

36. Ibid., p. 141.

37. Ibid., p. 90.

38. Hull, *Darwin and His Critics*, p. 412.

39. Darwin, *On the Origin of Species,* 1872, p. 70–71.

40. Peckham, *The Origin of Species: A Variorum Text*, p. 228.

41. Darwin, *On the Origin of Species*, 1872, p. 68.

42. Ibid., p. 178–180.

43. *Nature: A Weekly Illustrated Journal of Science*, vol. 23 (Nov. 11, 1880): p. 32.

44. Peckham, *The Origin of Species: A Variorum Text*, p. 349.

45. Ibid., p. 747.

46. Pamphlet: *Darwin and Christianity: Evolution Protest Movement* (United Kingdom: A.E. Norris and Sons, Ltd.).

47. L. Eiseley, *Darwin and the Mysterious Mr. X* (New York: E.P. Dutton, 1979).

48. Ward, *Charles Darwin: The Man and His Warfare*, p. 292.

49. Ibid., p. 322

50. Ibid., p. 307.

51. Ibid., p. 325

52. Ibid., p. 323.

53. A. Dupree, *Asa Gray* (Cambridge, MA: Harvard University Press, 1959), p. 340–341.

54. Himmelfarb, *Darwin and the Darwinian Revolution,* p. 88.

55. D. King-Hele, *Erasmus Darwin* (New York: Charles Scribner and Sons, 1963), p. 69.

56. Barlow, *The Autobiography of Charles Darwin*, p. 151.

57. Eiseley, *Darwin and the Mysterious Mr. X*, p. 46.

58. Ibid., p. 54.

59. Ibid., p. 46.

60. Ibid., p. 64.

61. T. Huxley, *Darwiniana: Reprint of the 1896 Edition* (New York: AMS Press, 1970), p. 475.

62. St. George Mivart, *On the Geneisis of Species* (New York: D.A. Appleton, 1871), p. 35.

63. A. Gray, "Critique of *The Origin of Species*," *The North British Review*, vol. 32 (1860).

64. C. Darwin, *On the Origin of Species* (New York: P.F. Collier & Sons, 1990), p. 243.

65. C. Darwin, *On the Origin of Species*, 1872, p. 222.

66. C. Darwin, *On the Origin of Species*, 1990, p. 20.

67. P. Feyerabend, *Against Method: Outline of an Anarchist Theory of Knowledge* (London: Humanities Press, 1978), p. 68.

68. K. Popper, *Objective Knowledge* (Oxford, UK: Clarendon Press, 1972), p. 265.

69. Himmelfarb, *Darwin and the Darwinian Revolution*, p. 318–319.

70. D. Kurtz, *Humanism Manifesto I and II* (Buffalo, NY: Prometheus Books, 1974), p. 8, 16.

71. C. Darwin, *The Origin of Species* (London: J.M. Dent and Sons Ltd., 1971), p. 167.

72. N. Gillespie, *Charles Darwin and the Problem of Creation* (Chicago, IL: The University of Chicago Press, 1979), p. 120.

73. Ibid., p. 15.

74. S. Gould, "Evolution's Erratic Pace," *Natural History*, vol. LXXXVI (5) (1977): p. 14.

75. Ibid., quoting Darwin.

76. J. Postlethwait and J. Hopson, *Modern Biology* (New York: Holt, Rinehart and Winston, 2006).

77. Gray, "Critique of *The Origin of Species*," p. 480.

78. Gillespie, *Charles Darwin and the Problem of Creation*, p. 15.

An Analysis of Darwin's Natural-Selection, Artificial-Selection Analogy

A s mentioned previously, the crowning achievement of Darwin's method of covert intimidation was his use of the natural-selection/artificial-selection analogy, whereby he used artificial selection as the mental stand-in for natural selection. The following essay describes how Darwin accomplished this mental sleight-of-hand and how this analogy can be revealed as false.

I also mentioned previously that Darwin should be regarded as a natural philosopher rather than an exact scientist. Darwin's *modus operandi* as an investigator was a throwback to the natural philosophical method of investigating the environment, which had been common among 17th-century naturalists and also prior to a reform of science instituted by René Descartes and Sir Francis Bacon, among others. It was characterized by: (1) an aversion to experimentation and observation because they lead to limited explanation and (2) a striving after unlimited explanation, which results in (3) an overloading of the facts far beyond what they can stand for. Exact science attempts to formulate truth statements about the environment; whereas when natural philosophy (4) makes statements about the environment, the main criterion is that they be philosophically or intuitively pleasing, hence there is inevitable bias. All of this adds up to pure speculation masquerading as science, and, because it is speculation, in order to convince others, the approach must necessarily be one of (5) persuasion rather than proof.

It was this natural philosophical methodology that caused Darwin embarrassment regarding the parallel-roads incident. Rather than acknowledging a conflicting fact in the lack of sea shells, he mongered in a hypothesis to explain that difficulty away. Years later he wrote that his parallel-roads hypothesis had been "one long gigantic blunder from beginning to end," and that, "my error has been a good lesson to me never to trust in science to the principle of exclusion."[1] Excluding alternative hypotheses is not a principle, but rather a corruption of science. Unfortunately, the lesson was not applied when he wrote *On the Origin of Species*. Special creation, or any alternative hypothesis similar in effect to special creation in relation to the evidences, is systematically excluded from consideration in favor of his *a priori* belief that life had evolved.

The Notion Suggested by Reading Malthus

At this point, we must review how the evolutionary natural selection hypothesis crystallized in the minds of both Darwin and Alfred R. Wallace. In January 1858 the natural selection hypothesis occurred to Wallace as follows:

> One day something brought to my recollection Malthus's *Principle of Population*. . . . I thought of his clear exposition of "the positive check to increase" — disease, accident, war, and famine. . . . It then occurred to me that these causes of their equivalence were continually acting in the case of animals also. . . . It occurred to me to ask the question, "Why do some die and some live?" . . . the best fitted lived . . . this self-acting process would necessarily *improve the race*.[2]

What one finds so interesting is that both men arrived at an identical hypothesis in an identical manner. It was immediately after reading, or thinking about, Thomas Malthyus's *Essay on the Principle of Population* that the idea of natural selection or survival of the fittest occurred to them. After reading Malthus's *Essay,* Darwin reports, "It at once struck me that favorable variations would tend to preserve, and unfavorable ones would be destroyed."[3]

Malthus was writing about the human population when he pointed out that populations tend to grow according to a geometric progression (e.g., double each generation), while food supply may be increased only to a limited extent. Famine becomes inevitable unless other catastrophes such as war and disease hold populations in check. Darwin and Wallace realized that the same potential for plant and animal populations to grow geometrically must also exist. What is holding their populations in check? The survival of the fittest: those with useful variations, such as length of neck, or wings or color, etc., survive the struggle and the others die out. The result is that populations are maintained at a level appropriate for the available food supplies, while an evolutionary change progresses.

But Does Selection Actually Occur in Nature?

Both theorists were confronted with the same problem — they could not prove that slight differences in a characteristic make a plant or animal more or less fit for survival. In other words, they could not report actually observing a variation being selected against and actually eliminated from a gene pool (the word, of course, is newer) of a species. Both theorists decided to use the same deceit. As a substitute for the unobserved natural selection, they make their hypothetical natural selection mechanism analogous to artificial selection.

Analogy Substituted for Observation

At this point, there is a parting of the ways in their thinking. The two theorists use their analogy differently. Artificial selection refers to the selection by man of domestic plants and animals in order to accentuate certain traits. Darwin's analogy goes something like this: if feeble man can make horses, for example, run faster by artificial selection, nature, being more powerful than man, could eventually change horses into new kinds of animals. He does not dwell on the fact that man only accentuates traits and does not create new kinds.

Wallace approaches the analogy this way: he concedes that man does not create new kinds by artificial selection. In fact, when domestic plants and animals are returned to their natural environment, they will either become extinct or return to their original condition. Somehow this was supposed to prove that natural selection could change organisms into new kinds.[4] In other words, plants and animals are immutable as far as artificial selection is concerned; seemingly illogical conclusions by both Darwin and Wallace.

What is the status of analogy among present-day logicians?

> Arguments from analogy may be fertile but they are all invalid.[5]

> Metaphors, like analogy, are dangerous, since they are double-edged.[6]

> It is unwise to stretch analogies too far. The results of our reasoning with analogy must be checked against reality to make sure that they hold.[7]

Although there is a legitimate tendency for people instinctively to think in terms of analogy, by relating the unknown to something familiar, it is being used in a false and misleading fashion when carried too far. Should we claim ignorance of the misleading potential of analogies for Darwin and excuse him on those grounds? No, the analogy is too skillfully and deliberately fashioned to have been written by someone who was naïve about their dangers. Darwin, I am convinced, knew the weakness of his argument when he wrote chapter IV in the *Origin*, where he introduced his alleged natural selection mechanism. For in the conclusion of the *Origin*, where he discusses whether life descended from four or five progenitors, or a single prototype, he makes this revealing comment: "But analogy may be a deceitful guide."[8]

Imagine, if you will, the enormous problem that confronted Darwin while writing the *Origin*: how could he convince the public that his mechanism, evolutionary natural selection, was really functioning in the environment when he could not report observing it in action? How could he convince people that the fit were surviving the competition and the less fit were being eliminated? Or more specifically, how could he convince people that nature had the selective power to eliminate absolutely some variations and to perpetuate others? It would be necessary for him to create an appearance of a mechanism and to hand this out to readers.

Let us make ourselves familiar with Darwin's method for making artificial selection the mental stand-in for evolutionary natural selection.

After discussing in the first three chapters topics such as selective breeding, variations under nature, and a struggle for existence caused by the potential for populations to increase geometrically, he introduces the natural selection mechanism in chapter IV. In the first three sentences he boldly begins making artificial selection analogous to natural selection. Chapter IV is about 36 pages long and has approximately 37 references making natural selections and artificial selections analogous. Here is a sample:

> Can it, then, be thought improbable, seeing that variations useful to man have undoubtedly occurred, that other variations useful in the same way to each being . . . should occur? . . . If such do occur, can we doubt . . . that individuals having any advantage . . . would have the best chance of surviving and procreating their kind?[9]

Frequent references to the artificial-selection/natural-selection analogy are made throughout the book. Here is one from chapter III: "I have called this principle, by which each slight variation, if useful, is preserved, by the term Natural Selection. . . . But the expression often used by Mr. Herbert Spencer of the survival of the fittest is more accurate . . . is a power incessantly ready for action, and is immeasurably superior to man's feeble efforts."[10]

Faced with this mental sleight-of-hand technique, the less critical reader is apt to accept artificial selection as proof of natural selection and not demand the obvious proof, which Darwin could not deliver: observation of the mechanism in action, in the environment.

Critique of the Analogy

As usually happens when analogies are applied, similarities are emphasized while differences are ignored. There are two things wrong with the natural-selection/artificial-selection analogy. First, man does not create new kinds by artificial selection; and second, we observe limited variability, not unlimited variability. Consequently, the analogy shows, if anything, that change from one kind to another kind would be impossible. It is one of the great ironies of this controversy, and it also demonstrates an ambivalence common among all of the founders of the evolutionary hypothesis, that Thomas Henry Huxley, Darwin's "bulldog," should be the one to reject Darwin's analogy and explicitly use artificial selection as a test against natural selection. His test is exact science; it places the burden of proof where it belongs, on the theorist. The evolutionists are required to prove that the unlimited variability that we do not observe, but which the hypothesis requires, does exist. Huxley's test reads as follows:

> Mr. Darwin, in order to place his views beyond the reach of all possible assault, ought to be able to demonstrate the possibility of developing from a particular stock by selective breeding, two forms, which should either be unable to cross one with another, or whose cross-bred offspring should be infertile with one another . . . it has not been found possible to produce this complete physiological divergence by selective breeding . . . if it should be proved, not only that this has not been done, but that it cannot be done . . . I hold that Mr. Darwin's hypothesis would be utterly shattered.[11]

Here we have a prime example of natural philosophical thoughts versus exact science supplied by the two leaders of the evolution movement. Darwin extrapolates as follows: if feeble man can make horses run faster by selective breeding, nature, which is more powerful than man, can transform horses into new creatures. Huxley does not buy the analogy, the extrapolation, or the relative strength or weakness of man and nature. He turns it against Darwin by proposing a test, which is to say that if man cannot create new kinds by artificial selection why should we think nature can? Weird, isn't it? Darwin, the author of the hypothesis, uses artificial selection to prove natural selection; while Huxley, the grand promotor of the views, turns it around and uses artificial selection to disprove natural selection.

Limitations to Artificial Selection

Considering the length of time that man has been selectively breeding plants and animals, not many people, even those favorably disposed toward evolutionary views, will harbor the belief that new kinds can be created by artificial selection. The hypothesis is disproved by the test. Huxley did not take this test lightly. He proposed it early in his career, and later in his book of essays on evolutionary hypothesis entitled *Darwiniana* he again makes special reference to it.

How did Darwin react to limited variability that would make evolution impossible? He simply ignored that conflicting fact: "That a limit to variation does exist in nature is assumed by most authors, though I am unable to discover a single fact on which this belief is grounded."[12] Darwin, like everyone else, observed limited variability, but imaginatively concluded unlimited variability.

Do Evolutionary Natural Selectors Exist?

Huxley and Asa Gray, the Harvard professor of botany, add a new dimension to the evolutionary natural selection hypothesis by questioning the existence of *natural selectors*. In this case it is not unlimited variability that is being questioned, but Darwin's assumption that nature, given unlimited variability, can select like man. In this quote Huxley describes the mechanism in a true Darwinian fashion.

> The Darwinian hypothesis . . . may be stated in a very few words; all species have been produced by the development of variety from common stock . . . by the process of natural selection, which process is essentially identical with that artificial selection by which man has originated the races of domestic animals.[13]

But then he becomes the skeptical scientist:

> Without the breeder there would be no selection, and without the selection no race . . . it must be proved that there is in Nature some power which takes the place of man, and performs a selection *sua sponte*.[14]

Man's efforts at selection are *consciously* directed. Can nature *spontaneously* do likewise? He later reiterates his skepticism.

> The question is, whether in nature there are causes competent to produce races, just in the same way as man is able to produce by selection such races of animals as we have already noticed.[15]

Gray, in the following quote, seems to be thinking along the same lines as Huxley: challenging Darwin's assumption, based upon analogy, that there is anything in nature that can select like man.

The assertions are, no doubt, backed by alleged facts; but almost every one of these "facts" gives occasion for controversy . . . the worth of these may be understood when we affirm, that Mr. Horner's Nile-Mud hypothesis is one of them. Besides . . . the views brought out in this chapter . . . are all associated with the presence of man's intelligence. But . . . it is not within the range of our belief, that, even though you affirm a personality to "Nature," while you banish God from the scene, this to some all-potent, *she*, would equal to these results.[16]

This throws a different light on alleged evolutionary natural selection; grant the hypothesis unlimited variability and useful-for-survival mutations, can nature select upon it? Can nature, like man, perpetuate some variations and eliminate others? If the reader will bear with me now, we can prove that evolutionary natural selection is naturally impossible, because there is nothing in the environment that can select like man.

Gray and Huxley seem to realize that artificial selection and the alleged evolutionary natural selection are two different entities, but to expose them as such is something they could not or would not do. The names themselves tell us that artificial selection cannot be analogous to natural selection; artificiality must, in fact, be the antithesis of naturalness.

What about Artificial Selection?

Artificial selection or selective breeding is really a technological endeavor. The dictionary gives this definition for technology: "the totality of the means employed to provide objects necessary for human sustenance and comfort." Technology is an effort by man to exploit or somehow utilize nature for his particular needs or desires. Artificial selection is a form, perhaps one of the oldest forms, of technology whereby man exploits the genetic variability of some domestic plants and animals to satisfy his needs or desires. In that sense, then, all domestic plants and animals are products of a technological effort, and consequently may be considered not natural but technological forms. They exist only so long as man is present to maintain them as technological products; remove man from the scene and technological organisms will revert to an original type.

Technological animals and plants are maintained under artificial conditions; man's presence is required to feed and protect them and above all make certain that varieties of the same kind are always inter-breeding. Golden retriever dogs, for example, only exist as long as man is present to make sure that they mate with their own kind; mongrels become a common variety when random mating is permitted.

Artificial selection, if the breeder is to acquire a degree of success, requires the rigid adherence to two basic rules. These rules are so simple and obvious that any breeder will instinctively apply them. Breeders do not need to be told what to do, although they may advise one another as to how best to accomplish their goals.

The Unwritten Rules for Artificial Selection

1. Prevent random mating of the selected individuals with individuals having undesirable traits. With animals, this usually requires some form of restraint such as pens or fences. With plants, the breeder may prevent undesirable cross-pollination by covering the pistil.

2. Prevent the random destruction of mature and immature individuals having the desirable traits.

The net result of the strict enforcement of these rules is to make man a persistent and consistent selector with the ability to make micro-changes in certain desirable directions. The failure to enforce these rules is to prevent any change and to preserve the status quo. Success requires a constant enforcement of the rules. A breeder cannot expect to make any progress if for several generations horses are bred up for speed and then for even one generation are allowed to mate indiscriminately. The persistence and consistence required by artificial selection may be illustrated by the British, who at one time had a law requiring the destruction of all horses under a certain size. This, of course, was to ensure an increase in horse size.

Darwin claims this for his mechanism: "It may metaphorically be said that natural selection is daily and hourly scrutinizing, throughout the world, the slightest variation; rejecting those that are bad, preserving and adding up all that are good; silently and insensibly working, *whenever and wherever opportunity offers*, at the improvement of each organic being in relation to its organic or inorganic conditions of life."[17]

First Analogy, Now Metaphor

The reader will notice that Darwin claims that Nature is selecting only in a *metaphorical* sense. In other words, Nature is not literally selecting for some traits and eliminating others; natural selection is merely a figure of speech. Darwin elaborated on this when he wrote: "In the literal sense of the word, no doubt, natural selection is a false term." He goes on to say that "everyone knows what is meant and is implied by such metaphorical expressions; and they are almost necessary for brevity. . . . I mean by Nature only the aggregate action and product of many natural laws, and by laws the sequence of events as ascertained by us." He closes by assuring the reader that this is nothing to be concerned about: "With a little familiarity such superficial objections will be forgotten."[18]

In regard to natural selection as a metaphor, Macbeth notes the following: "If the reader is surprised to find natural selection disintegrating under scrutiny, I was no less so. But when we reflect upon the matter, is it so surprising? The biologists have innocently confessed that natural selection is a metaphor, and every experienced person knows that it is dangerous to work with metaphors. As the road to hell is paved with good intentions, so the road to confusion is paved with good metaphors. Perhaps the sober investigator should not have staked so much on a poetic device."[19]

What does all of this mean: suddenly to learn that natural selection is merely a figure of speech, a poetic metaphor? In Darwin's definitions of natural selection, we obviously were led to believe that nature was in a literal sense preserving and eliminating variations. We were further led to believe this by a carefully calculated effort to make natural selection analogous to artificial selection. In a literal sense, there is artificial selection: man does preserve some variations and eliminate or at least suppress others with his constant vigilance.

What is the status of metaphors in scientific method? It is acknowledged that they are not applicable; they are as useless and dangerous as analogies (which, of course, they resemble). Metaphors have a literary value, but are useless in science. They are, in fact, a throwback to the natural philosopher's desire for total explanation:

Any theories based on metaphors are highly hypothetical.[20]

Metaphors, like analogies, are dangerous, since they are double-edged. While they have a legitimate heuristic use, and are also suggestive, the suggestions they make are often the source of errors which would otherwise have been avoided.

Metaphorical Statements are not true or false, but merely apt or inapt, appropriate or inappropriate. Scientific statements make truth claims and therefore cannot be metaphorical.[21]

Also, "to mistake the metaphorical for the fact is to be the victim of the metaphor, and this is perhaps only another way of saying that we must not accept the metaphor as true."[22] And, "an unresolved metaphor consists of a false ('nonsensical') identification or attribution."[23]

It all comes down to this: evolutionary hypothesis, allegedly one of the greatest scientific theories of all times, the foundation for many philosophies, religions, and political systems, is merely a metaphor "proved" by an analogy, an abomination of science. Those who believe it have been over-influenced by the clever persuasion tactics of a natural philosopher.

Analysis of the Natural-Selector, Artificial-Selector Analogy

It is within the capability of scientific analysis to prove the impossibility of evolutionary natural selection. Science, as we have learned, takes words in a literal sense; therefore, in order to bring natural selection into the realm of science we must find a way to analyze it in a literal sense.

Whenever anyone uses the phrase "natural selection" or when we read in a book that this or that organ or organisms evolved by means of natural selection, the speaker or writer is really using a cliché to express his ignorance. Natural selection is supposed to be comprehended by analogically associating it with artificial selection. The writer or speaker understands literally, exactly, and specifically how man, the selector, accomplishes his tasks, but cannot literally, exactly, and specifically describe the factors or forces in nature that allegedly accomplish its task. Natural selection is comprehended metaphorically and analogically, not literally. Let us prove now what Huxley and Gray suspected: that there is nothing in nature that can select as man can.

To do this, we must reduce both artificial selection and evolutionary natural selection to the same common denominator. Failure to do this has permitted this false analogy to live. When the phrase "artificial selection" is used, we immediately identify man as the *selector*. Man's success as a selector, although limited by limited variability, is a result of his being a persistent and consistent selector. A desultory, haphazard, random selector would merely preserve the status quo. And we know that man is a persistent and consistent selector because he has the intelligence to enforce the two basic rules of artificial selection, which is really a form of technology.

The problem comes when we use the phrase "natural selection." We have permitted evolutionists to identify nature, or the environment, as the selector analogous to man. But nature is a connotation too vague and ephemeral for scientific use; it represents an "aggregate" of alleged selectors. In order to overcome this incorrect comparison, we must do with the phrase "natural selection" what we have done with the phrase "artificial selection," namely identify and specify the selector.

You may recall that the real test for evolutionary natural selection would be to observe it in the environment. As a substitute for observation, Darwin made the mechanism seem analogous to artificial selection while proposing imaginary examples. Direct observation, however, would make analogy and imagination unnecessary.

Imaginary Examples of Natural Selection

Let us analyze his imaginary examples and reveal how unrealistic they are. The first one is an example of macroevolution, how Darwin thought bears could be transformed into whalelike animals: "In North America the black bear was seen by Hearne swimming for hours with widely opened mouths, thus catching, like a whale, insects in the water. Even in so extreme a case as this, if the supply of insects were constant, and if better-adapted competitors did not already exist in the country, I can see no difficulty in a race of bears being rendered, by natural selection, more and more aquatic in their structure and habits, with larger and larger mouths, till a creature was produced as monstrous as a whale."[24]

As explained earlier, whether the analogy is true or false can only be determined by identifying the selector in the environment. The selector in the example just described is the insects in the water. Man has only accomplished microevolution in his selection; but according to Darwin's analogy, the insects, functioning spontaneously, can transform bears into whalelike animals! The example may seem ridiculous, absurd, and fantastic in the highest degree, but according to evolutionary hypothesis it would be a commonplace occurrence.

I maintain that the insects are not persistent and consistent selectors like man, and to entertain the idea that they are is unreal. Darwin admits, "In the case of methodical selection, a breeder selects for some definite object; and if the individuals be allowed freely to intercross, his work will completely fail."[25] There is no way that the insects can prevent random mating of ordinary bears in the territory with the bears that are supposed to evolve. Insects cannot enforce the first rule of artificial selection and consequently cannot make any changes in the natural status quo, which is a phenotype of bears, some with slightly larger or smaller mouths and bears with ordinary paws and bears with incipient (very slightly) finlike paws. The exceptionally large mouths and fins, even if we concede that such dramatic traits can occur, would have to begin as incipient forms and, because of random mating, could never develop into anything of any survival advantage. Man, as a persistent and consistent selector, must be constantly vigilant; while the insects, according to the analogy, are supposed to accomplish more than man by simply being passively in existence in the water.

Macroevolution, the change from one kind to another, is what we are challenging. Macroevolution would require unlimited variability as well as a persistent and consistent selector. It is interesting to note that the bear to whalelike transformation was the only example of selection involving macroevolution that I could find. This example was in the first edition of the *Origin*, but Darwin was advised to remove it, probably because it put too much strain on the credibility of the hypothesis. Yet, according to the views, the example should be considered commonplace. In the remaining editions of the *Origin*, the example was revised to read as follows: "In North America the black bear was seen by Hearne swimming for hours with widely opened mouth, thus catching, almost like a whale, insects in the water."[26] As you can see, the second important sentence is omitted and the reader is left to imagine that the sentence that remains is some sort of evidence for evolution.

The remaining examples of selection that will be analyzed, some of which have actually been observed, apply to microevolution, a change within a kind, the possibility of which is not being questioned, when man is the selector. But even this seems to be more than any natural selector can accomplish. Artificial selection, to achieve microevolution, is a technological technique and seems to be more than a natural selector can duplicate. We are not challenging selection *per se*. Some sort of selection must be holding the populations in check; but it is not evolutionary natural selection, leading to macro changes.

Darwin imagined that giraffes acquired long necks because it was a survival advantage for food-getting. Critics of this imaginary example pointed out that if long necks are of significant survival advantage, why do we not have a large number of quadrupeds with long necks? Darwin could only answer with vague conjecture.

The example of how giraffes are believed to have acquired a long neck is given in most of the high school textbooks. It is illustrated in a series of pictures to compare Darwin's hypothesis with Lamarck's defunct views. Lamarck, according to the pictures, would say that giraffes *needed* a long neck and, by stretching their necks to reach the vegetation, their offspring would somehow end up with longer necks.

According to Darwin's hypothesis, the first picture shows several giraffes, some with long necks and some with shorter necks. The second picture shows long-necked giraffes feeding while on the ground lies a dead giraffe, presumably a starved short-necked one. The third and final picture shows several uniformly long-necked giraffes. The alleged example creates more questions than it answers. For example, it does not explain how all giraffes originally would have come to have necks long enough to make slight differences in lengths a survival factor.

When we analyze these pictures in class, I ask the students what the natural selector is and they tell me it is the vegetation. I ask them if they think the lack of vegetation can eliminate short-necked giraffes — they think not. They seem to think that the amount of available vegetation at lower levels would always be sufficient to sustain short-necked giraffes; therefore, the status quo of the first picture would have been preserved. Vegetation is a random factor, the quantity and availability of which may vary from place to place and time to time. The randomness of the factor forbids it from ever being a persistent and consistent selector. It would ever and always permit mating of short-necked giraffes with long-necked giraffes.

On at least two occasions students have commented, and several authors have pointed out also, that if the lack of low vegetation could rigorously destroy adult short-necked giraffes, then the offspring from the long-necked giraffes would also be rigorously destroyed. We see immature giraffes surviving after being weaned and can assume than that short-necked adult giraffes could also. The example disintegrates under close analysis.

Sometimes a student will suggest in reply that perhaps long-necked adult giraffes pull vegetation down to within range of their offspring. The student has a perfect right to formulate that hypothesis but should realize that he or she is simply mongering-in an hypothesis with no basis in fact, as a natural philosopher would do, to save the hypothesis.

May I reiterate that besides limited variability, evolutionary natural selection is impossible because according to Darwin's own analogy, no natural selector can eliminate some traits and perpetuate others. Natural selectors can only preserve the genotypic status quo or temporarily alter it. This is exemplified in the following example from the *Origin*: ". . . of the best short-beaked tumbler-pigeons a greater number perished in the egg than are able to get out of it. . . . Now if nature had to make the beak of a full-grown pigeon very short for the bird's own advantage . . . there would be simultaneously the most rigorous selection of all the young birds within the egg, which had the most powerful and hardest beaks . . . or more delicate and more easily broken shells might be selected."[27]

This example of selection involving microevolution reveals Darwin's lack of mental rigor as a theorist. We see also how Darwin personified nature, giving it the capability to make decisions like man. In this example he suggests that nature can determine at the embryonic stage what kind of beak would be useful for birds as adults. The natural selector in this example is the hardness of the egg shell. Obviously, egg shells cannot eliminate one kind of beak and perpetuate another kind. He plainly states that the thicknesses of the egg shells vary at random (not persistently and consistently) as do kinds of beaks. Well then, if the selector varies at random and the trait varies at random, the status quo will be preserved and no change will occur in any direction. We have here a perfect example of the randomness that seems to pervade nature. Nordenskiold explains it this way: "The variations are certainly guided by laws . . . not, however, in any given direction but in all possible directions, and they are influenced, depending upon every chance, quite incalculably by natural selection. But if, then, natural selection were guided by chance it would exclude the possibility of any law-bound phenomenon in existence. Herein really lies the greatest weakness of the Darwinian Doctrine of selection."[28]

This example of selection involving microevolution occurred about the turn of the century in England. A Professor Bumpus collected a sampling of sparrows of the species *Passer domesticus*, which were killed during a February sleet and snow storm. Measurements were made of the weight, length of beaks and skulls, length of humerus, etc. The general conclusion from the study was "that when nature selects, through the agency of winter storms of this particular severity, those sparrows which are short stand a better chance of surviving."[29]

The selector in this example is the February storm. Obviously, it is not a persistent and consistent selector. In fact, the inconclusive results of this study could not be verified because of the infrequent occurrence of that kind of storm in a given area. Storms rarely occur in consecutive years in the same areas and of comparable severity. The storm may have temporarily altered the genotypic and phenotypic status quo in an isolated area, but random mating of the surviving sparrows within that area and possibly the surrounding areas will prevent a micro-change to smaller sparrows.

The Much-Mentioned Peppered Moth

When I ask students to check the literature for examples of evolutionary natural selection, they frequently cite the example of the moths near Manchester, England. Evolutionists have gotten a great deal of mileage out of this study, and on the surface it appears to be a valid example. The actual results, however, prove what has been concluded from the other examples, that natural selectors cannot select persistently and consistently as man can. The selectors fail because they cannot eliminate one trait while preventing random mating.

This study was conducted in the 1950s by Dr. H.B.D. Kettlewell. Back in the 1800s it was noted that there was a dark pigment and a light pigment form of the peppered moth *Biston betularia*. The phenotypic status quo in the vicinity of Manchester in 1848 was about 1 percent of the dark form to 99 percent of the light form. This ratio was believed to be the result of birds preying on the moths as they rested on the lichens growing on the bark of the trees in the woodland. The dark moths were more conspicuous against the light background of the lichens, so they were eaten most frequently.

As a consequence of industrial development, the natural habitat was altered by soot and chemical gases from the factories so that the bark of the trees in these areas was darkened. Conditions were now reversed: the light moths had the pigment that was most conspicuous. At the time Kettlewell conducted his study in the 1950s, the dark moths had become the dominant phenotype.

The natural selectors in this example are the birds that prey upon the moths. In the unpolluted habitat the birds apparently were unable to eliminate the dark moths, probably because there were always enough dark areas on the tree bark where dark moths would tend to rest and become inconspicuous. In the polluted habitat where man actually, inadvertently but nevertheless, was co-selector with the birds, the light moths could not be eliminated. Probably the reason was the same as that given for the unpolluted habitat; also there would be a continual movement of light-colored moths into the area from adjacent unpolluted areas.

Recent environmental concern has brought about a reduction in the amount of soot and gases that formerly polluted the area. Predictably, the tree bark has returned to its natural color, and the ratio of dark to light moths is again being reversed. One thing is certain: the natural selectors were unable, in either the natural or the artificial habitat, permanently to alter the genotypes of moths in any one direction.

Now, if man were to eliminate one form of the peppered moths by artificial selection, he would have to isolate a portion of the population to prevent random mating with migrating moths and then systematically remove all offspring over many generations having the undesirable color. Theoretically, the desired form would breed true as long as the artificial selection persisted.

In these analyses we have made careful distinctions in order to avoid gross assumptions. It is a blatant deception for evolutionists to claim any kind of selection as evolutionary natural selection when it obviously falls short of what the hypothesis requires.

Speculation vs. Fact about Wolves

The following quote from the *Origin* is another imaginary example of selection involving microevolution that explained, to those who wanted to believe it, how wolves became swift and agile. The example also demonstrates the advantage scientific observation has over natural philosophical speculation. It is unique in that what Darwin imagined can be contrasted with actual observation.

> Let us take the case of a wolf, which preys on various animals, securing some by craft, and some by strength, and some by fleetness; and let us suppose that the fleetest prey, a deer for instance, have from any change in the country increased in numbers. . . . Under such circumstances, the swiftest and slimmest wolves would have the best chance of surviving and so be preserved or selected. . . . I can see no more reason to doubt that this would be the result, than that man should be able to improve the fleetness of his greyhound by careful and methodical selection.[30]

In this example, Darwin, true to form, attempts to make it credible by analogically comparing it to man's selection of greyhound dogs. The selector in this example is the swiftness of the deer. Although wolves feed on other prey, the reader is left with the impression that the deer-wolf/prey-predator relationship is of evolutionary importance. If one were to carry this example to its logical conclusion, the wolf would in turn be considered a selector to make deer faster by eliminating the slower ones. The wolves would not then be gaining an advantage from an increased speed, since, hypothetically, every slight increase in speed on the part of the wolves would be offset by an increase in the speed of the deer.

Now let us discover what is really happening in the great outdoors. In the late 1950s Farley Mowat, a trained biologist, was sent by the Canadian government into the Arctic region to determine the cause of a rapid depletion of the caribou herds. Mowat concluded that wolves, the prime suspects, were not the cause, but more likely overzealous hunters were. He became intimately familiar with a wolf family, and was able to study their habits closely and even to learn how wolves hunt their prey. Contrary to what Darwin speculated, slight differences in speed among the caribou were not of any significance, since the slowest healthy caribou could easily outdistance a wolf. Wolves instead select their prey on the basis of vigor versus infirmity.

Mowat learned that a healthy adult caribou, and even a three-week-old fawn, can easily outrun a wolf. Knowing it was a senseless waste of energy to attempt to run down a healthy caribou, the wolves would rather systematically test the state of health of the deer in order to find one that was not up to par. This was done by rushing each band and putting them to flight. If an inferior beast was not revealed, they would give up the chase and test another band.[31]

When the testing finally revealed an inferior beast, "the attacking wolf would . . . go for its prey in a glorious surge of speed and power . . . the deer would begin frantically zigzagging . . . this enables the wolf to take shortcuts and close the gap more quickly."

Mowat also reports, "Most of these carcasses showed evidence of disease or serious debility . . . on a number of occasions I reached a deer almost as soon as the wolves had killed it. . . . Several of these deer were so heavily infested with external and internal parasites that they were little better than walking menageries, doomed to die soon in any case."[32]

From this observed example of selection we learn that it has no evolutionary significance. There is no way that deer can eliminate the genes for slowness in the gene pool of wolves. Randomness is the overriding factor in the deer-wolf/prey-predator relationship. It is not a life or death struggle, as Darwin imagined, slight differences in speed determining the outcome. The slowest wolves can participate and share in a kill equally with any slightly faster wolves among the pack. The genotype of the pack is preserved. Apparently under the sun, the race is not to the swift nor the battle to the strong, but time and chance happen to them all (Eccles. 9:11).

The wolf predation actually benefits the caribou herd; it results in the maintenance of a high reproductive vigor among the caribou by eliminating the diseased and aged members who would consume food but probably would not reproduce.

A similar study was conducted of the moose-wolf/prey-predator relationship on Isle Royale in Lake Superior. An analysis of the skeletal remains of wolf-killed moose revealed that in this instance also the wolves were taking individuals that were old and arthritic. Selection was based upon vigor versus infirmity, not upon variations in speed.

Any Selection in Nature Is Commonly Random

Let us pass on to one final example of alleged evolutionary natural selection. This example deals with the common snail, *Cepaea nemoralis*, which is frequently preyed upon by thrushes. The shells of the snails are colored dark brown or pinkish or yellow (greenish when the animal is within). To this colored surface up to five blackish bands may be added. A study of shell remains revealed that "they destroy relatively few of the least conspicuous types; yellow (greenish) upon grass; brown upon leaf litter in woods; banded shells upon a diversified background, as mixed herbage; and unbanded in a relatively uniform environment." The author says that the thrushes do not select at random, but in the next paragraph states, "Yet though the inappropriate colours and patterns are constantly being eliminated in nature, the populations do not become invariable."[33]

Obviously, the selection was random to a degree that one or more colors or patterns could not be eliminated. The thrushes could not cause microevolution. How could they? The snails are constantly moving, the backgrounds are constantly changing, seasonally and from place to place, and the snails are randomly mating. A color or pattern that was favored at one time and in one area may not be so in another area at a different time. The author attributes the persistent variability of colors and patterns, not to the randomness of the thrushes as selectors, but the genetic make-up of the snails — a supergene that resists the elimination of a trait, which only adds to the numerous objections already confronting the alleged mechanism.

Summary of the
Natural-Selector/Artificial-Selector Analogy

We have now completed an analysis of the alleged evolutionary natural-selection mechanism. We have noted that it fails the test of observation and have gone on to explain that natural selectors lack the persistence and consistence necessary to favor one variation to the exclusion of others. You may recall that Darwin's mechanism was developed as follows:

Fact 1. Variations exist — no two members of a species are exactly alike.

Fact 2. Populations *tend* to increase geometrically — e.g., 2, 4, 8, 16, 32, 64, etc.

The salient question, then, is what is holding populations in check? Darwin's answer was the evolutionary natural selection mechanism. But because of limited variability, lack of useful-for-survival mutations,[34] random selectors, and a failure to observe the mechanism in action, Darwin's guess as to what is holding the population in check must be incorrect. Conversely, because of limited variability, lack of useful-for-survival mutations, and successful observation of random natural selection in action, random natural selection, at least random to the degree that traits are not eliminated, must be what is holding populations in check. Therefore, this alternative to Darwin's hypothesis should be included in the textbooks.

What is holding populations in check?
3. No selectors in nature can choose to eliminate some variations and perpetuate others.
4. Random selection holds populations in check, resulting in no macroevolution (observed).

Now I know evolutionists will insist that both kinds of selection, random natural selection and evolutionary natural selection, are occurring in the environment. In fact, Darwin has already conceded random selection.

> There must be much fortuitous destruction, which can have little or no influence on the course of natural selection. For instance, a vast number of eggs or seeds are annually devoured, and these could be modified to natural selection only if they varied in some manner which protected them from their enemies. Yet many of these eggs or seeds would perhaps, if not destroyed, have yielded individuals better adapted to their condition of life than any of those which happened to survive . . . a vast number of . . . animals and plants, whether or not they be the best adapted to their conditions, must be annually destroyed by accidental causes.[35]

The point is that we have no reason at all to believe that his alleged evolutionary natural selection plays a part in holding populations in check, and every reason to believe that fortuitous destruction or random natural selection is the only kind of selection that is functioning in the environment. In other words, a double standard exists; the evolutionary natural-selection mechanism is credible according to natural philosophy but is disproved according to exact science.

What Difference Does Time Make?

In closing, it may be appropriate to consider the question of time available for evolution. Darwin confused the issue by relating infinite power for evolution to infinite time. Consequently, the concept of an extremely old earth is regarded by less rigorous thinkers as proof of evolution. Radiometric dating, which is supposed to indicate an old earth, is, however, a procedure open to question. If, for example, someone reports that a fossil or rock stratum is approximately 100,000 years old, one can only accept that date on the conviction that the test itself was conducted without error, and that the rate of radioactive decay has always been constant throughout time. There is no way to cross-check a date that old with the only logical test involving human witness — recorded history. An extremely old earth would not, indeed, in itself prove evolution. On the other hand, a young earth would be another factor disproving evolutionary views. Other than that, the concept of time is not relevant to the hypothesis. Besides, several authors have pointed out that parts of an organism are correlated; therefore, organisms cannot change slowly, but would have to come into existence *en bloc* or not at all. So the gradual accumulation of variations, supposedly shrouded in the mists of time, is an impossibility even though eternity were granted. Also, the random relationship presently observed between natural selectors and variations could never have been a persistent and consistent relationship in the past, even an infinite past. A random relationship between selector and variations is the law-bound phenomenon in our environment. The concept of immense time is no defense of or evidence for an alleged mechanism that is obviously not functioning at the present time.

Endnotes
  1. F. Darwin, *The Life and Letters of Charles Darwin,* Vol.1 (New York: Appleton and Co., 1887), p. 69.
  2. H. Ward, *Charles Darwin: The Man and His Warfare* (Indianapolis, IN: The Bobbs-Merrill Co., 1927), p. 288.

3. Ibid., p. 225.

4. G.E. Brosseau, *Evolution* (Dubuque, IA: William C. Brown Co., 1969), p. 29–38.

5. W.H. Leatherdale, *The Role of Analogy Model and Metaphor in Science* (New York: American Elsevier Publishing Co., 1974), p..205

6. Ibid., p.181

7. H. Ruchlis, *Clear Thinking* (New York: Harper and Row, 1962), p. 151.

8. C. Darwin, *The Origin of Species and the Descent of Man* (New York: The Random House, Inc., 1872), p. 370.

9. Ibid., p. 63.

10. Ibid., p.52

11. T.H. Huxley, *Darwiniana* (New York: AMS Press, Inc., 1970), p. 463–464, reprinted from the 1896 edition.

12. F. Darwin, *Foundations of the Origin of Species* (Cambridge, England: Cambridge University Press, 1909), p. 109.

13. Huxley, *Darwiniana*, p. 71.

14. Ibid., p. 17.

15. Ibid., p. 433.

16. A. Gray, "The Origin of Species," *The North British Review*, Vol. 1860, 32:465.

17. Darwin, *The Origin of Species and the Descent of Man*, p. 66.

18. Ibid., p. 64.

19. N. Macbeth, *Darwin Retried* (Boston, MA: Gambit, Inc., 1971), p. 50.

20. Leatherdale, *The Role of Analogy Model and Metaphor in Science*, p. 206.

21. Ibid., p. 181.

22. Ibid., p. 149.

23. Ibid., p. 102.

24. C. Darwin, *On the Origin of Species* (London: John Murray, 1859), facsimile printed by the Harvard University Press, Cambridge, MA, 1966, p. 184.

25. Ibid., p. 78.

26. Ibid., p. 131.

27. Ibid., p. 68

28. E. Nordenskiold, *The History of Biology* (New York: Tudor Publishing Co., 1928), p. 470.

29. Brosseau, *Evolution*, p. 62–66.

30. Darwin, *On the Origin of Species*, p. 70.

31. F. Mowat, *Never Cry Wolf* (New York: Dell Publishing Co., Inc., 1963), p. 142.

32. Ibid., p. 145–146.

33. J.J. Head and O.E. Lowenstein, editors, *Evolution Studied by Observation and Experiment* (London: Oxford University Press, 1973), p. 10.

34. R.R. Hedtke, "Darwin, Mendel and Evolution: Some Further Considerations," *The American Biology Teacher*. 36(5):310-1, 1974.

35. Darwin, *On the Origin of Species*, p. 68.

Chapter III

Asa Gray and Theistic Evolution

Recently, some paleontologists have advanced a hypothesis called "punctuated equilibria" in an attempt to bring the gaps in the fossil record into conformity with their belief in evolution. According to this idea, evolution occurred rapidly at times, thus explaining the sudden appearance of more complex kinds of plants and animals and the lack of transitional fossils. What the mechanism was for this alleged rapid evolution they do not know. Essentially, punctuated equilibria proponents have retreated to pre-Darwinian evolution, at which time there was no credible mechanism; one was expected to accept evolution on faith. I personally do not think punctuated equilibria will gain wide acceptance in the scientific community because of its lack of a credible naturalistic mechanism and the feeling that the idea is somehow a little too contrived.

The odd thing about punctuated equilibria is that it was originated by Asa Gray, who called it theistic evolution. The difference being that, rather than an unknown mechanism, the mechanism was the work of God.

In this essay are discussed the scientific evidences that prompted Asa Gray to try to persuade Charles Darwin to adopt theistic evolution and Darwin's reasons for rejecting theistic in favor of atheistic evolution. In their arguments, both men appealed to the fossil record. Besides their interpretations of that record, the one by Georges Cuvier is mentioned, and it is noted that yet others are possible. So various alternative interpretations of the record are considered, to see which one best fits the facts.

Proponents of theistic evolution should realize that their point of view, for good reason, was never seriously considered by the founders of the evolutionary hypothesis — except for Asa Gray. Theistic evolution, if not originated, was at least avidly promoted by this Harvard professor of botany. Theistic evolution or the design principle (evidence of intelligent design in nature) attempts to include theism while not excluding evolution. It is an attempt to incorporate both *a priori* systems.

In a private letter, Gray explains his position as follows: "Since atheistic doctrines of evolution are prevailing and likely to prevail, more or less, among scientific men, I have thought it important and have taken considerable pain to show that they may be held theistically."[1] And in an anonymously written article, Gray explains his position similarly: "It would not be dealing fairly by our readers, and, especially, it would be unmindful of the apologetic value of natural theology, were we to look at this hypothesis from any other point of view, than the twofold one of science and theology."[2]

Gray was not without influence, and he used it to try to persuade Darwin to adopt theistic evolution. Briefly stated, his argument for design goes like this: Did Darwin mean to exclude theism entirely? Gray had been comforting Americans by pointing out how Darwin recognized divine purpose, citing, for example, the three quotations that Darwin had posted in the front of the *Origin* — two from theologians and one from Bacon — which emphasized "Divine power," "intelligent agent," and "book of God's word."[3]

If Darwin does not mean to exclude theism, why not assume that the Creator directed the evolutionary process? Gray described his concept of theistic evolution metaphorically as "streams flowing over a sloping plain (here the counterpart of natural selection) may have worn their actual channels as they flowed; yet their particular course may have been assigned; and where we see them forming definite and useful lines of variation, after a manner unaccountable in the laws of gravitation and dynamics we should believe that the distribution was designed."[4] John Dewey, one of the founders of the progressive education movement, aptly described Gray's theistic evolution as "design on the installment plan. If we conceive the 'streams of variations' to be itself intended, we may suppose that each successive variation was designed from the first to be selected."[5]

Needless to say, as the textbooks will verify, Gray's "design on the installment plan" was rejected by Darwin. In a private letter, Darwin informed Gray of the rejection: "If the right variation occurred, and no others, natural selection would be superfluous." Himmelfarb describes Darwin's rejection in more detail: "For if each variation was predetermined so as to conduce to a proper end, there was no need for natural selection at all. The whole point of his hypothesis being that, out of undesigned and random variations, selection created an evolution pattern."[6] Publicly, Darwin rejected Gray's argument for theistic evolution, when on the last page of *Variation of Plants and Animals Under Domestication* he concluded, "However much we may wish, we can hardly follow Professor Asa Gray in his belief in lines of beneficient variation."[7]

Darwin, of course, could not admit supernatural intervention if he was to have natural selection be the great thing that he wanted it to be. If the Creator periodically introduced streams of beneficent variations, that is, useful variations that were preordained to accumulate into new kinds, in a miraculous way, this was really a slowed-down version of special creation. Dupree reports that Gray had to pay for his insistence on the design principle: "With Darwin's decision against the design argument, Gray lost his place as a shaper of strategy within the inner circle of friends."[8] It mattered little to Gray if theistic evolution made natural selection superfluous; he thought the mechanism was overrated anyway.

> We believe that species vary, and that "natural selection" works; but we suspect that its operation, like every analogous natural operation, may be limited by something else. Just as every species by its natural rate of reproduction would soon completely fill any country it could live in, but does not, being checked by some other species or some other condition — so it may be supposed that variation and natural selection have their struggle and consequent check, or are limited by something inherent in the constitution of organic beings.[9]

Similarly, Gray states:

> The organs being given, natural selection may account for some improvement; if given of a variety of sorts or grades, natural selection might determine which should survive and where it should prevail.[10]

This, you may recall, is the original concept of natural selection, as proposed by Edward Blyth, namely, that it was a conservative rather than a creative mechanism. This is also where Darwin ended his revision of natural selection, particularly when he conceded that it was incompetent to account for the development of incipient organs. Continuing the same line of thought, Gray again states:

> If it be true that no species can vary beyond defined limits, it matters little whether natural selection would be efficent in producing definite variations.[11]

Gray felt that Darwin's hypothesis was inadequate to explain the origin of life. Even if one were to concede that the natural selection mechanism works, the hypothesis would still require a mechanism to provide correlated variations for selection. Natural selection does not create variations.

Gray's theistic evolution was more than an effort to save the creation concept while including evolution; it was also an hypothesis based upon the data from geology and paleontology. It was an effort to explain the fossil record that to him was inexplicable in terms of special creation or atheistic evolution. The stringing-out of the fossils from simple to complex indicated, contrary to special creation, a coming into existence of new life forms at successive periods in the earth's history. On the other hand, the absence of intermediate fossils, although compatible to special creation, contradicts atheistic evolution. Gray describes it this way:

> Why, it is asked, do we not find in the earth's crust any traces of transitional forms? The lame answer is that "extinction and natural selection go hand in hand." In other words, traces of the higher forms exist, but the transitional ones, having served their ends, are lost! You might as well say that, when in after ages the site of a battle between the Caffres and British shall be disturbed, there will be found only the traces of the superior,

conquering race. But it will not do to plead imperfection of the geological record. If any data may be relied on in this question, those supplied to us by the paleontologist may be so.

The truth is, that if the author has wholly and signally failed to produce even one unquestioned corroborative proof of true transitional variety among present forms of life, he cannot discover material in the geological record for a chapter on transitional varieties in paleontology. But while we shall not ask our readers to survey the fossiliferous deposits, there are two subjects we wish to refer to ere we close. These are the question of breaks in the introduction of life, and the question of miraculous action.[12]

From the very outset, even before the publication of the *Origin*, Gray, aware of its contents, could not reconcile the lack of intermediate forms with Darwin's development hypothesis. To Joseph Hooker he wrote, "Assume the extinction of any quantity of intermediate forms and you can then imagine the development of the present vegetable kingdom by excessive variation. But just consider what an enormous amount of sheer, gratuitous assumption this requires!"[13]

Even T.H. Huxley, "Darwin's bulldog," was compelled to agree with Gray about the fossil record.

> What does an impartial survey of the positively ascertained truths of paleontology testify in relation to the common doctrine of progressive modification? It negatives these doctrines; for it either shows us no evidence of such modifications, or demonstrates such modification as has occurred to have been very slight; and, as to the nature of that modification, it yields no evidence whatsoever that the earlier members of any long-continued group were more generalized in structure than the later ones.[14]

For Gray, then, the breaks in the introduction of life can be explained by miraculous action.

> The question of the presence of miracle, at various points in the history of the earth, is one which has been, with a strange want of logic, almost universally regarded by eminent men

with suspicion. Why? We suppose very few, if any, not even excepting Mr. Darwin, would be willing to deny that there has been the exercise, at some period of the earth's history, of creative power — in a word, miracle. But if you acknowledge its presence at any one point, why be suspicious of it, or deny its probability, at any after-point in the history? If in every respect you find that what demanded a miracle at A, is again found existing at E, after having ceased to be before it again made its appearance, first at B, second at C, and third at D, is there anything to forbid the conclusion, that at every one of these stages there was miraculous action?[15]

Cuvier's Views Contrasted with Gray's

It would be well to digress for a moment and consider Georges Cuvier's attempt to solve the riddle of the fossil record. The reader should be aware that Cuvier, one of the most influential men in science in his day and the founder of paleontology, was writing prior to the publication of the *Origin*, yet at a time when the idea of evolution or the transformation of life preoccupied many men in science, and while Sir Charles Lyell's uniformitarian geology was gaining wide acceptance over catastrophic geology. Cuvier, like Gray, could not reconcile the absence of intermediate fossils with evolutionary views:

> He based his entire refutation upon the incompleteness of the fossil record. If the fossils could not show us the course of the supposed transmutations, what reason was there to believe that these unusual events had actually occurred? The fossils were our only record of life in the remote past, and their lesson was obvious and not at all, Cuvier believed, what the transformists would have liked it to be. Not a continuous series of almost similar creatures but rather an interrupted sequence of dissimilar forms was what was discovered. "We may," said Cuvier, "respond to them (transformists) in their own system that, if the species have changed by degrees, we should find some traces of these gradual modifications; between the paleotherium and today's species we should find some intermediary forms: this has not yet happened."[16]

Whereas Gray's attempt to solve the riddle of the fossil record was "progressive," Cuvier's was "extinctive." As Coleman describes it:

His system was, if anything, "extinctive," eliminating by catastrophe, and not "progressive," creating (through God) new and higher creatures as an aftermath of catastrophe. There had been a succession of discrete populations, each more or less complete, and each nearly perishing by the action of some remote catastrophe.[17]

Nordenskiold makes this clarification about Cuvier's catastrophic geology:

The assertion that so often occurs in literature that, in his view, life had been created anew after each catastrophe is utterly incorrect; on the contrary, he points out that isolated parts of the earth may have been spared on each occasion when it was laid waste, and that living creatures have propagated their species anew from these cases, which indeed he expressly applies to the human race.[18]

As the reader may have gathered, Cuvier's explanation of the fossil record required the rejection of uniformitarian geology which Coleman describes as follows:

Rain, snow, and ice, Cuvier admitted, do attack and wear away the mountains and hills, but this argument assumed "the pre-existence of mountains, valleys, and plains, in a word, all the inequalities of the world, and consequently could not have given rise to these inequalities." Sedimentation could produce no major changes in the level of the sea, whatever minor changes were known being either still in question or purely local phenomena. Volcanos, the principle factor in the Huttonian [James Hutton, who preceded Lyell in advancing the idea of uniformitarian geology] system, generated curious and extensive local upheavals profoundly changing the surrounding countryside but not, Cuvier believed, disturbing the adjacent strata. Astronomical causes such as comets or precession were equally rejected. Cuvier concluded that all of these forces lack the strength and generality which, judged by the effects, are required and that "it is in vain that one seeks, in the forces presently acting on the surface of the earth, causes sufficient to produce the revolutions and the catastrophes the traces of which its surface discloses to us."[19]

Nordenskiold describes Cuvier's catastrophic geology this way:

> He at once takes it for granted that these changes had the character of violent catastrophes; that they were violent he considers to be established by the fact of stratifications which, judging from the nature of the fossils, have demonstrably taken place in the sea, are now found on the one hand elevated to enormous heights and on the other hand overthrown and inverted. That all this took place with great rapidity is obvious to his mind, not only from the sharp lines of demarcation shown by the various strata, but also from the fact that many of them contain such extraordinarily numerous animal remains that it can only be assumed that they died a sudden death as the result of upheavals which obliterated all life [in some areas?] for the time being.[20] [Comment added.]

Needless to say, Cuvier's series of catastrophes is not the brand of geology preferred by either the atheistic evolutionists or the special creationists.

The Various Theories Contrasted

What all of this condenses down to is that Gray had made the fossil record explicable at the high cost of destroying all previously formulated evolution theories. Gray's "design on the installment plan," as Dewey described it, was, more specifically, "creation on the installment plan." Theistic evolution is not really evolution at all. Cuvier had made the fossil record explicable at the expense of both the evolutionist's uniformitarian geology and the special creationist's flood geology, meaning a single, worldwide catastrophe.

From Gray's, Cuvier's, and Huxley's points of view, the atheistic evolutionists, if their hypothesis was to be credible, would have to produce large numbers of intermediate fossil forms as predicted by the hypothesis or formulate an hypothesis based upon facts to explain their absence; otherwise, it is in violation of a well-established axiom in science that states, "A single absolute conflict between fact and hypothesis is fatal to the hypothesis; *falsa in uno, falsa in omnibus.*"[21]

Likewise, the special creationists are obliged to explain the stringing-out of the fossils from simple to complex compatibly with their point of view.

Let us review briefly what has been learned concerning the fossil record: it is not possible for the same evidence to at once refute and support an hypothesis. The absence of intermediate fossils is prime evidence against evolutionary views; and it is the responsibility of evolutionists to prove the existence of such forms or formulate a credible hypothesis based upon facts to explain their absence. It is not the critic's responsibility to try to prove a negative. Evolutionists have failed in this responsibility, yet the hypothesis that they defend has not had to bear the full weight of this conflicting fact, because the stringing-out of the fossils from simple to complex is "as it should be." The net result is that the conflicting fact appears not to be as serious as it should be. Nevertheless, we are still left in the impossible situation of having the same evidence at once both support and refute an hypothesis.

Relative Fossil-Production Potential

An hypothesis that could possibly explain the stringing-out of fossils from simple to complex based upon creation rather than evolution is Relative Fossil Production Potential (RFPP). This hypothesis is explained in more detail elsewhere, but a brief explanation is relevant at this point.

The qualitative equation goes like this: Quantity of Fossils Produced = Habitat + Population Size + Size and Structure. Ostensibly, the fossil record reveals the sequence in which organisms evolved into existence, but, in reality, according to RFPP, it reveals an ecological-geological fossilization phenomenon. Generally speaking, the so-called simple kinds have greater likelihood of producing more fossils than the so-called complex kinds. Consider, if you will, the fossilization potential of clams as compared to camels, which represent opposite ends of the fossil record.

The factors that determine fossil production cannot be applied to the various kinds of plants and animals in any mechanical law-bound sense, but it is obvious nevertheless that variations in fossil production potential must exist. For example, fishes must have a greater RFPP than most reptiles, and the RFPP of algae must be greater than most land plants. Whereas RFPP predicts a tendency for fossils to be strung-out, the evolutionary interpretation of the fossil record is a law-bound prediction; it is obliged to reveal a stringing-out of the fossils from simple to complex, as well as intermediate kinds of fossil. Contrary to the prediction, the fossil record has revealed many anomalies from the viewpoint of evolutionary progression, which, on the other hand, are predictable according to RFPP. The Lewis "overthrust" in Montana is frequently cited as an example. In this area, "Pre-Cambrian" rocks (rocks that are characterized by an absence of distinguishable fossils, making them even older than the "Cambrian" rocks that contain invertebrate fossils) are lying above "Cretaceous" rocks that allegedly are of the period when reptiles evolved.

Another example that contradicts the evolution interpretation of the fossil record, but serves to demonstrate RFPP, is the discovery of pollen grains from Angiosperm and Gymnosperm trees in "Pre-Cambrian" rocks. Flower-producing plants and cone-producing trees were not supposed to have evolved for hundreds of millions of years after the "Pre-Cambrian" rocks were laid down. Which has the greatest RFPP — pollen grains or the trees that produce them? Applying the factors in the qualitative equation, the pollen grains, which are produced like dust in the air, must have a population size millions of times greater than the parent trees; and their tiny size, with a covering that is somewhat resistant to decomposition, lends itself to deposition and preservation in sediment. Couple these two factors to a widespread wind-blown habitat, and it is conceivable that the pollen would be discovered in "Pre-Cambrian" rocks while the contemporaneous parent plants may have become part of the "Carboniferous" coal strata that evolutionists believe to be millions of years younger.

Many more out-of-sequence anomalies have been reported that may be considered evidence for flood geology rather than uniformitarian geology. For this reason, the RFPP concept originally was based upon flood geology, yet I would be committing an error common to the natural philosophers, that is, overloading the hypothesis, if I were to insist the RFPP, in itself, is proof of flood geology and can only be considered in reference to flood geology. RFPP is a fact about our environment and must be considered regardless of what one's brand of geology may be. RFPP is applicable to either uniformitarian or catastrophic geology. Evolutionists, it would seem, are obligated to incorporate RFPP, a relevant fact, into their interpretation of the fossil record. If they would, my thinking is that it would be sufficient, especially when also considering the conflicting fact of the absence of intermediate fossils, to account for the stringing-out of fossils and make the evolution interpretation superfluous.

Summary: The Hypotheses Compared

Let me summarize, as I see them, the merits and weaknesses of the various hypotheses that pertain to the fossil record. Asa Gray's theistic evolution hypothesis, that life came into existence at consecutive periods in the earth's history, has the virtue of explaining the stringing-out of fossils and predicts no intermediates. Its drawback seems to be that the stringing-out from simple to complex is law-bound; consequently, it does not explain the anomalies where fossils are found out of sequence, with no evidence of overthrust.

Georges Cuvier's hypothesis, based, apparently, upon special creation and a series of catastrophes, might explain the stringing-out and certainly predicts no intermediate fossils. Out-of-sequence fossils are not an anomaly to his hypothesis; it is predictable that they could occur.

Charles Darwin's evolution hypothesis accounts for the stringing-out of fossils, but is contradicted by the lack of numerous intermediate fossils that it predicts should be found. Also, it is hampered by the law-bound prediction that fossil remains will be found in sequence from simple to complex as they supposedly evolved into existence.

The final hypothesis, based upon special creation and relative fossil production potential, explains the stringing-out and predicts no intermediate fossils. The stringing-out is not law-bound; therefore, out-of-sequence anomalies are predicted, or at least allowed. Its advantage, though, is that it takes into consideration a fact of life that the other hypotheses do not incorporate, namely, that some kinds of organisms have a greater potential for leaving a greater quantity of fossil remains than others.

Of the four hypotheses, Darwin's evolution hypothesis seems to be the least likely candidate, even though it is the only hypothesis presently in the textbooks. The quotes contained in this article reveal how the history of evolutionary views has been distorted and unwanted parts suppressed in the popular textbooks. As a result, over the years evolution views have become scientific dogma; consequently, the mindset for most people is to think of it philosophically, when, in reality, it is a scientific statement about our environment that does not agree with the facts.

Note: I quoted from two articles anonymously published in the *North British Review* in 1860 and 1867; Darwin attributes the authorship of the 1860 article to a Rev. Mr. Dunns and identifies Fleeming Jenkin, a British engineer and inventor, as the author of the 1867 article. He also refers to the article in the sixth edition of the *Origin* but does not venture publicly to name Jenkin.

I located the articles in Poole's *Index to Periodical Literature*, Vol. I, 1802–1881, listed under the name of Asa Gray. In the preface to the index, Poole testifies to having reliably identified the authors of anonymous articles published in the *North British Review*. I find Gray's essays on evolutionary hypothesis in *Darwiniana* (T.H. Huxley also wrote a book of essays entitled *Darwiniana*) compatible with the anonymous articles in the *North British Review*.

Also, in a letter to the editor in *Nature* magazine, we see the similarity of thought between it and those published in the *North British Review*, regarding limited variability. The article was published under Gray's name in 1883; this was about one year after Darwin's death. The gist of it reads as follows:

> Fairly is it said that "the theory merely supposes" this. For omnifarious variations is no fact of observation, nor a demonstrable or, in my opinion, even a warrantable inference from observed facts. It is merely an hypothesis to be tried by observation and experiment.

He concludes:

> The upshot is, that, so far as observation extends, it does not warrant the supposition of omnifarious and aimless variation; and the speculative assumption of it appears to have no scientific value.

Darwin's position on the question of limited variability or unlimited variability (alleged useful-for-survival mutations being the sources of variability) was diametrically opposed to Gray's position: "That a limit to variation does exist in nature is assumed by most authors, though I am unable to discover a single fact on which this belief is grounded."

Endnotes

1. A.H. Dupree, *Asa Gray* (Cambridge, MA: Harvard University Press, 1959), p. 359.

2. A. Gray, "The Origin of Species," *The North British Review*, 32:456 (1860).

3. H. Ward, *Charles Darwin: The Man and His Warfare* (Indianapolis, IN: The Bobbs-Merrill Co., 1927), p. 321.

4. Dupree, *Asa Gray*, p. 297.

5. J. Dewey, *The Influence of Darwin on Philosophy* (New York: Peter Smith Co., 1951), p. 12.

6. G. Himmelfarb, *Darwin and the Darwinian Revolution* (London: Chatto and Windus, 1959), p. 286.

7. C. Darwin, *The Variations of Animals and Plants under Domestication* (New York: AMS Press, 1896), p. 428.

8. Dupree, *Asa Gray*, p. 301.

9. A. Gray, *Darwiniana* (Cambridge, MA: Harvard University Press, 1963), p. 110–111.

10. A. Gray, "Review of Darwin's Theory on the Origin of Species by Means of Natural Selection," *The American Journal of Science and Arts* 29(86):179 (1860).

11. A. Gray, "The Origin of Species," *The North British Review*, 46:317 (1867).

12. Gray, "The Origin of Species," p. 481.

13. Dupree, *Asa Gray*, p. 265.

14. Himmelfarb, *Darwin and the Darwinian Revolution*, p. 272.

15. Gray, "The Origin of Species," p. 486–487.

16. W. Coleman, *Georges Cuvier — Zoologist — A Study in the History of Evolution Theory* (Cambridge, MA: Harvard University Press, 1964), p. 150.

17. Ibid., p. 151.

18. E. Nordenskiold, *The History of Biology* (New York: Tudor Publishing Co., 1928), p. 338.

19. Coleman, *Georges Cuvier — Zoologist*, p. 131.

20. Nordenskiold, *The History of Biology*, p. 338.

21. W.S. Jevons, *The Principles of Science — A Treatise on Logic and the Scientific Method* (New York: Dover Publications, 1958), p. 516.

Chapter IV

A Geo-Ecological Explanation of the Fossil Record Based upon Divine Creation

This essay, originally published in 1970, is an attempt to explain why fossils are strung out simple to complex in the earth's crust in a way that is compatible to special creation. To find simple fossils like invertebrates in the deeper rock strata and complex fossils like mammals in upper rock strata is as it should be for evolutionary views; conversely, the lack of intermediate fossils is not as it should be for evolutionary notions.

One would think that if all life were miraculously created at approximately the same time, we would find both simple and complex fossil remains mixed together in the various rock strata. Creationists explain the stringing-out of the fossils from simple to complex as resulting from the hydrodynamics or sorting process of flood geology, believing the rock strata to have been rapidly deposited. Evolutionists do not recognize flood geology and explain the string-out as the order in which organisms evolved into existence, believing the rock strata to have been deposited slowly over immense periods of time, as proposed by Lyell.

Available Fossils

Two important facts must be pointed out regarding fossil formation. The first is that nearly all fossil evidence is found in a particular type of rock called sedimentary rock. Sedimentary rocks are formed when particles or minerals originating from the break-down of rocks are swept into bodies of water such as lakes or oceans. These particles settle out as unconsolidated sediments that later harden into true rocks. Because of this process of settling out of water, sedimentary rocks have the distinguishing feature of being layered or stratified.[1] There are other sources of fossil remains such as amber, glaciers, tar pits, etc., but these sources are relatively rare. We will deal, then, only with fossils found in sedimentary rocks, as do all paleontologists, with the rarest exception.[2]

The second fact is that a prerequisite for the formation of any fossil formed in sedimentary rocks is that very soon after the death of an organism, it becomes buried. To remain exposed, whether on land or in water, soon results in the destruction and decomposition of the organic tissue by scavengers and microorganisms.[3]

Rapid burial in sediment is a necessity in the formation of fossils and has a direct bearing upon the fossil production potential of any group of organisms. Not all organisms have an equal likelihood of leaving fossil remains. Because of certain ecological and environmental conditions, some groups of organisms have a greater chance of being fossilized in greater number than do other groups of organisms. We may refer to this index as the relative fossil-production potential of a species, a factor that must be considered in any explanation of the fossil record.

Although fossils may have been formed to some small extent in minor floods, it is reasonable to believe that most of the sedimentary deposits were found during the global flood known as the Noachian deluge. With rapid burial in sediment the primary requirement for the formation of a fossil, any organism in any niche of the pre-Flood community might possibly have left fossil remains. It is obvious also that organisms living in an aquatic or semiaquatic habitat would have been under optimum conditions for fossil production during the Flood, since they would have been most likely to sink into or become covered with advancing sediments.

Other Fossil-Formation Difficulties

When considering fossil land animals such as the reptiles, birds, and mammals, additional difficulties in fossil formation are encountered. When these animals were buried, most of the carcasses would have been first scattered and destroyed by scavengers and micro-organisms.

Uniformitarian geologists largely agree, stating that terrestrial organisms may not be buried at all *unless a sudden flood or freshet occurs which may also have the effect of scattering the remains still more.*[4] Proximity to water, then, would have provided a greater RFPP for aquatic organisms in the deluge than for terrestrial organisms.

Another factor to consider in determining the RFPP of a group of organisms is their population size. If all other factors influencing the RFPP of two groups of organisms were equal, the group with the largest population size would have produced the greatest quantity of fossil remains. Smaller organisms generally have the greatest population sizes. This is true because the smaller creatures require less space and energy from the ecosystem than the larger ones, and therefore a larger number of niches are available for them.[5]

A third factor, morphology, should be considered, although its effect in determining RFPP may have been minimal. By morphology, I mean the kind and quantity of tissue making up the body structure. Size and structure as factors in fossilization would have had a much more important application to land organisms than aquatic organisms, because the opportunity for rapid burial is not as great for land organisms. This is true now and was probably also true during the Flood event.

Remains of a terrestrial organism with a large amount of hard tissue probably would have survived decomposition longer than one with a small amount of hard tissue, thus increasing the chances of fossilization. On the other hand, a small quantity of tissue requires less sediment in which to become buried! Apparently, either an extremely large size or an extremely small size could be beneficial in fossil production.

An example as to how structural composition may influence RFPP comes from palynology — the study of pollen grains. Fossil evidence of pollen grains and microspores may be quite abundant in some rock strata, while evidence of the parent plants in the same stratum is completely absent. Population size alone could account for this phenomenon, since the number of pollen grains must be millions of times greater than that of the parent plants. But an additional influencing factor may be that the outer walls of spores are especially resistant to decomposition.[6]

One must conclude that the extent of the specific influence of the size and structure factor upon the RFPP of a group of organisms is difficult to determine.

Habitat, population size, and size and structure of the organism are the three main factors that influenced the relative fossil-production potential of the pre-Flood groups of organisms. It can be summarized in the following qualitative equation:

Habitat + Population Size + Size and Structure = RFPP

For example, a creature that was near the water, that came from a large population, and that was structurally resistant to decay would have been more readily fossilized than one that was terrestrial, from a small population, and/or had a structure prone to decay.

Application of Relative Fossil-Production Potential upon Index Fossil

In the fossil record, many organisms are often referred to as index fossils. They include the following groups of organisms: insects, fishes, mammals, invertebrates, reptiles, protozoans, amphibians, and birds. If the above equation is applied to the index organisms, we can determine the RFPP for each group and compare it to their stratigraphic arrangement in the fossil series.

Using the first factor, *habitat*, the groups may be arranged in a column with those in or nearest water at the bottom.

PRIMARILY TERRESTRIAL	PRIMARILY AQUATIC
birds	amphibians
mammals	protozoans
insects	fishes
reptiles	invertebrates

Notice that the column can be divided into two convenient groups — those that are primarily aquatic and those that are primarily terrestrial. These two groups should be given separate consideration in any further rearrangement because the groups that are primarily aquatic would have had a definite advantage in fossil production over the groups that are primarily terrestrial. Their vertical order in this sequence (sometimes called the "principle of faunal succession") could thus relate to their proximity to bodies of water before the Flood and not to the supposed long ages of fossil history.

Applying the next factor, *population size*, the column may be rearranged as follows with descending order from least to most easily fossilized:

	INDEX FOSSILS	NUMBER OF KNOWN SPECIES
Primarily terrestrial	mammals	4,500[7]
	birds	9,000[8]
	reptiles	5,000[9]
	insects	800,000[10]
Primarily aquatic	amphibians	2,000[11]
	fishes	30,000[12]
	invertebrates	236,000
	protozoans	30,000[13]

After each index group the number of known species is recorded. No one could possibly know the exact population sizes for these groups before the Flood, but the number of species known at present may serve as an index of their relative population sizes. The interpretation of population size is, of course, the larger the population size the larger the quantity of fossils produced in the Flood and now available for discovery. (It should be pointed out that the figure for the known species of invertebrates includes the following phyla: Porifera — 5,000 sp.,[14] Coelenterata — 9,000 sp.,[15] Arthropoda — [except Class Insecta] 91,000 sp.,[16] Echinodermata — 6,000 sp.,[17] Mollusca — 100,000 sp.,[18] Annelida — 15,000 sp.,[19] and Platyhelminthes — 10,000 sp.[20] Only the more commonly known phyla were included in arriving at the total number of species of invertebrates.)

Two Discrepancies Noted

There are two discrepancies in the arrangement of these groups according to population size in comparison to their arrangement in proximity to water, and that is in the placement of protozoans and reptiles. Both groups immediately above these two have larger numbers of known species.

There are two reasons why protozoans should possibly be left where they are despite the fact that fewer protozoan species are known than other invertebrates. First, because they are microscopic in size, greater opportunity exists for them to become more numerous in the ecosystem than any of the other organisms listed, even though fewer species are recognized. Second, many species of protozoans may not as yet have been discovered as pointed out in the following quotation from a noted zoologist:

> The number of named species of Protozoa lies somewhere between 15,000 and 50,000, but this figure probably represents only a fraction of the total number of species. Some proto-zoologists think that there may be more protozoan species than all other species together.[21]

The second discrepancy involves placement of reptiles before birds. The ultimate advantage in fossil production is a close proximity to water. Generally speaking, reptiles may be more closely associated with water than birds. Also in this particular situation, the third factor, *size and structure*, may make a difference. Reptiles have a tough scaly skin and some of them, like the extinct dinosaurs, had massive bone tissue; whereas birds are generally quite fragile in structure. They have no tough outer skin except on their legs, and much of their bone structure is hollow to provide for easier flight. The size and structure factor coupled with the habitat factor could raise the RFPP of reptiles above that of birds.

The index fossils are now arranged in an order according to their relative fossil-production potential. The greatest RFPP is at the bottom of the column and the least RFPP is at the top (see figure 1). The horizontal width of the band for each index group indicates its RFPP, which is to say the quantity of fossils available for discovery.

It is significant and meaningful to note that the index fossils are now arranged according to the fossil record and that the concept of evolution has been *completely dismissed* in arriving at this arrangement. Instead, the principle of relative abundance and proximity to water (RFPP) before the Flood has been used.

Determining Relative Fossil-Production Potential of Specific Organisms

Difficulties may be encountered when attempting to stratigraphically arrange specific kinds of organisms, rather than large representative groups, according to the RFPP factors. These difficulties are due

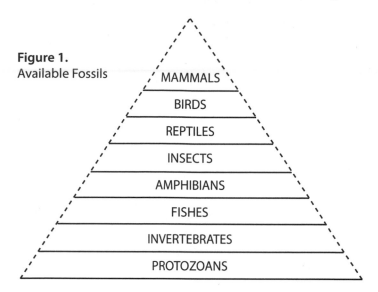

Figure 1.
Available Fossils

to a lack of obvious differences in the RFPP factors among some of the organisms involved.

Let us work out the stratigraphic arrangement of the following kinds of organisms that have been related to specific rock strata: shark, cockroach, opossum, crocodile, horseshoe crab, and *Bairdia* (a tiny marine arthropod).[22]

The immutability of these organisms cannot be satisfactorily explained in evolutionary terms.[23] Fossil evidence of these organisms dates back to rock strata supposedly millions of years old; yet they have remained apparently unchanged up to the present, according to the uniformitarian frame of reference.

These organisms also contradict the following statement by Charles Darwin: "Judging from the past, we may safely infer that not one living species will transmit its unaltered likeness to a distant futurity."[24] These organisms have transmitted their unaltered likeness to a distant futurity.

Beginning with the *habitat* factor, the above-mentioned organisms may be arranged as follows:

PRIMARILY TERRESTRIAL	PRIMARILY AQUATIC
6. opossum	1. horseshoe crab
4. cockroach	3. shark
5. crocodile	2. *Bairdia*

The organisms have been numbered to indicate the way they should be arranged stratigraphically from bottom to top according to historical geologists. The habitat factor alone brings about a rough semblance of order in that the organisms numbered 1, 2, and 3 are at the bottom half of the column and organisms numbered 4, 5, and 6 are at the top half, which is stratigraphically correct so far.

A judgment in the current or past difference in the *population sizes* of opossums and crocodiles is difficult to make. If the opossum population was and is greater than that of the crocodile population, it apparently has been overshadowed by the semiaquatic habitat of the crocodile, resulting in a greater RFPP for the crocodiles during the Flood.

Conversely, the population size of cockroaches, an insect, is overwhelmingly larger and more widely distributed than that of either crocodiles or opossums, resulting in their having the greatest RFPP of the three primarily terrestrial organisms. One should also remember that, although insects are small in *size*, they are not fragile. Their tough exoskeleton often results in unusually complete fossils.[25] The additional influence of the population factor could rearrange the primarily terrestrial organisms in their proper stratigraphic sequence — cockroach, crocodile, opossum.

Turning to the three organisms that are primarily marine, one would have to assume that sharks, a considerably larger organism than either the horseshoe crab or *Bairdia,* would have the smallest population size of the three, resulting in a lower RFPP. When considering the horseshoe crab and *Bairdia*, it is easy to determine why they would have a greater RFPP than all of the other organisms being compared, but due to the lack of a significant difference in any of the RFPP factors, it is difficult to determine, between the two, which has the greatest RFPP. Perhaps the rate at which sediment was deposited in the marine environment had an effect upon the RFPP of some organisms.

The following list shows the accepted stratigraphic arrangement and the geological period of the organisms we have been considering.

6. Opossum — Cretaceous
5. Crocodile — Triassic
4. Cockroach — Pennsylvanian
3. Shark — Devonian
2. *Bairdia* — Ordovician
1. Horseshoe crab — Cambrian

Available Rocks

It is obvious when examining the fossil record that there is not much direct evidence to support creation. There is considerable indirect evidence in that many "gaps" exist. The various groups of animals or plants appear in the strata as if they had no evolutionary ancestry.

Yet inevitably the question arises, "If all organisms were created during creation week, why do we not find evidence of higher forms of life in the oldest rock strata?" The answer may rest upon the difference in the quantity of fossils produced by various groups of organisms as previously discussed. It is comparatively easier to find a million needles (protozoans) in a hay stack than it is to find one needle (mammals).

The quantity of fossils partly answers the question, but one must turn to some basic geology for additional factors. Fossil production is of no use in studying the past if the rocks in which the fossils are located are not available for examination. The quantity of available rocks determines the variety of fossils that can be discovered.

Sedimentary rocks are formed in layers, and the strata formed first in the Flood are at or near the bottom, while those formed later are at or near the top. This stratification of sedimentary rocks makes random sampling difficult because the deeper layers are more inaccessible than the upper layers. In fact, in order to be available for extensive study, deep strata must be uplifted and exposed to the surface.[26]

Accessibility of rocks deserves serious consideration. For example, if the deep rock strata can be examined only to a limited extent because of their inaccessibility, then the kinds of fossil remains one will most likely find will be the kinds that are most abundant, the protozoans, invertebrates, etc., not birds and mammals. Conversely, one *can* find the comparatively rare fossils in the last-formed or more accessible strata. These upper strata can be examined more thoroughly.

To say that it is all simply a matter of chance that one cannot find the higher forms of life in the deeper strata may not by itself be a convincing argument. One should realize, however, that after a fossil has formed, it may not necessarily remain indefinitely available for discovery because the environment in which the sedimentary rocks were formed may change, thus changing the rocks and the fossils in them. This is pointed out by a noted geologist.

Some of the rocks now visible on the surface of the earth were once buried as deeply as ten miles down. Under such conditions of extreme pressure and heat many common minerals, especially those of sedimentary rocks, are subject to change, being stable only within a limited range of rather low pressure and temperature. Under deep burial or in other parts of the crust where unusually high temperatures or pressures prevail or where hot magmatic fluids can affect them, these minerals tend to change, slowly without melting, into other minerals more stable in the new environment. These changes are called metamorphism.[27]

From this one may deduce that the deeper, first-formed layers of sedimentary rocks were changed since the Flood by the process of metamorphism. If the rocks were changed, what about the fossils in them?

Some metamorphosed rocks retain as relicts the original structures of the parent rocks. Pebbles in a conglomerate, for example, may be preserved in the metamorphosed rock, but each pebble is usually distorted and stretched out. Fossils, too, tend to be deformed (broken or stretched) in the rare cases where they are preserved in the metamorphosed sedimentary rocks.[28]

So fossils are rarely found in deep metamorphosed rocks because they were destroyed or, if not destroyed, distorted.

Uniformitarians hold that the oldest strata of rocks were formed during what is referred to as the Pre-Cambrian period. One author writes that it is difficult to study about Pre-Cambrian rocks because of:

. . . the general concealment of overlying, younger rocks. In addition, most Pre-Cambrian rocks have existed long enough and been buried deeply enough to have been metamorphosed and deformed, thus destroying or altering original mineral composition, sedimentary or igneous structures, and other evidence of former conditions.[29]

If deep fossils have been destroyed by metamorphism since the flood, then the kinds of fossils that most likely would have survived the process, and also been left as fossil evidence, would have been from organisms that had the greatest RFPP.

One other point should be made regarding fossil destruction, namely, that even if a deep stratum of rock does become uplifted or somehow exposed to the surface, it and the fossils in it may have been removed by erosion.[30]

In summary, primarily two factors, accessibility and metamorphism, determine the quantity of rocks available for examination. I propose another qualitative equation:

Accessibility + Metamorphism = Available Rocks

The strata of rocks first formed are generally more inaccessible and more likely to have become metamorphosed than strata of rocks formed last. The quantity of unmetamorphosed and easily accessible upper strata of rocks should be much greater than that of deeper strata. This is illustrated in the triangle in figure 2.

As stated previously, if examination of strata formed first in the Flood is limited because of inaccessibility and metamorphism, one would most likely find only the fossil remains of organisms with the greatest RFPP. If examination of strata formed later in the Flood is less limited by inaccessibility and metamorphism, one would find fossil remains of organism with a low RFPP as well as a high RFPP. This is illustrated by superimposing the available rocks triangle over the available fossils triangle as in figure 3.

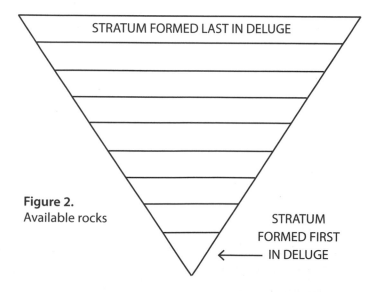

Figure 2.
Available rocks

STRATUM FORMED LAST IN DELUGE

STRATUM FORMED FIRST ← IN DELUGE

Figure 3. The fossil record reinterpreted

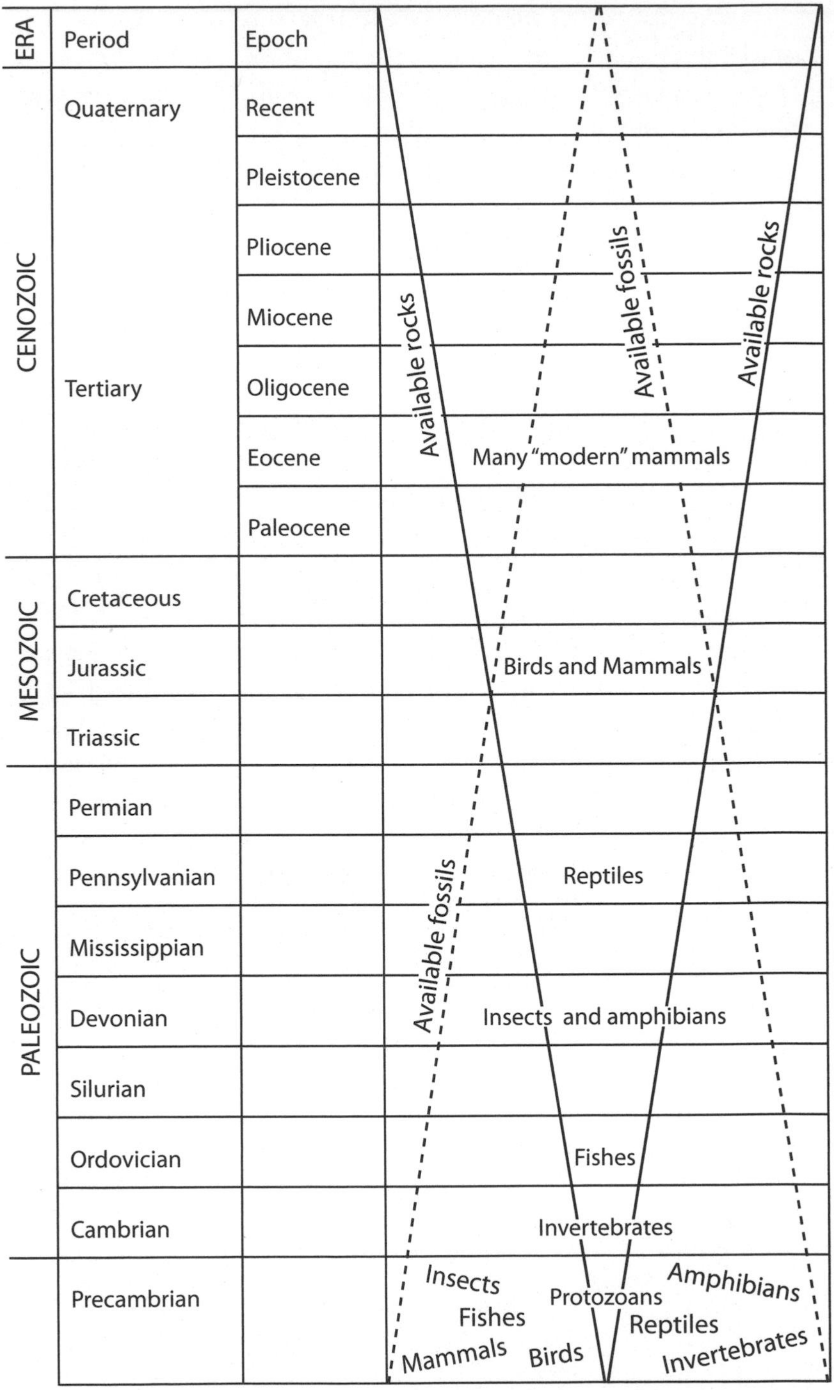

ERA	Period	Epoch			
CENOZOIC	Quaternary	Recent			
		Pleistocene			
	Tertiary	Pliocene		*Available rocks*	*Available fossils* / *Available rocks*
		Miocene			
		Oligocene			
		Eocene		Many "modern" mammals	
		Paleocene			
MESOZOIC	Cretaceous				
	Jurassic			Birds and Mammals	
	Triassic				
PALEOZOIC	Permian				
	Pennsylvanian			Reptiles	
	Mississippian			*Available fossils*	
	Devonian			Insects and amphibians	
	Silurian				
	Ordovician			Fishes	
	Cambrian			Invertebrates	
	Precambrian			Insects Fishes Mammals Birds Protozoans Amphibians Reptiles Invertebrates	

Interpretation of the Triangles

All of the index organisms existed when the Pre-Cambrian rocks were formed either before the Flood or in its earliest stages. Only fossil remains of protozoans are found in the Pre-Cambrian rocks, *not* because they evolved prior to the rest of the index organisms, but because they have the greatest RFPP of all the index organisms, while the quantity of available sedimentary rocks is at a minimum in that stratum.

And so it is with each of the index fossils. Fossil remains of insects are not discovered until the so-called Devonian period, because the RFPP or quantity of fossil evidence of insects along with the quantity of available rocks made discovery possible at that particular stratum and not a deeper stratum. A third equation encompasses these ideas:

Available Fossils + Available Rocks = Known Fossil Record

Notes on the Fossil Record

It has been estimated that the fossil record that we have today (an accumulation of fossil discovery since the 18th century) may represent no more than 1 percent of the possibly ten million species of plants and animals that may be preserved in rocks.[31] That being the case, and if this explanation of the fossil record is correct, one would expect, as more rocks are examined, a gradual shift downward in the stratigraphic arrangement of the fossil evidence. Over the years, that has been the trend. Thus many organisms may have lived at an *earlier* date than was once believed. The following organisms are a few examples of that trend.

1. **Neocalamites** (Equisetales) — Remains of this plant were previously known from the Devonian to the end of the Paleozoic. This reference reports them as being found in upper Triassic age strata, although most of the remains are very fragmentary. It will be noted that in this case the stratigraphic range is extended upward.

2. **Ogygopsis** (a trilobite genus) — Heretofore known in the Mid-Cambrian and now extended downward to the upper part of the Lower-Cambrian of the Canadian Rockies region.

3. **Eryops** (a labyrinthodont amphibian) — The stratigraphic range of this animal has been extended from the Permian down into the Pennsylvanian period.

4. **Anisus pattersoni** (a freshwater snail) — Earlier restricted to the Pleistocene; now found in the upper Pliocene epoch as well.

5. **Sphenodontids** (reptiles of Triassic period) — Footprints of this reptile have now been found in Triassic period sediments, and the author contends it is only a matter of time until true fossil remains are uncovered.

6. **Early Seed Plants** (Gymnosperms) — These are plants characterized by naked seeds and include the seed ferns, conifers, and cycads. Reference is made here to the fact that the gymnosperms first appeared in the early lower carboniferous periods some 250 million years ago. However, the reference states that it will not be surprising if the gymnosperms eventually are traced back to the underlying Devonian period. The author states that the first generally accepted flowering plants have been found in the mid-lower Cretaceous, but fossils that have been attributed to this group come from the Jurassic and Triassic, and a few botanists have expressed the opinion that they originated as far back as the Permian.

It is apparent from the above data that the changes involving the stratigraphic position of fossils are of minor magnitude, for the most part. In other words, the first appearance of a particular fossil may be shifted downward on the time chart from one epoch to the next older epoch or from the upper horizons of one geologic system to the mid-portions of the same system. It is questionable whether shifts involving several periods by virtue of a single new discovery will be encountered. However, as new discoveries continue to be made, this slow displacement may result in a time span of considerable magnitude.[32]

The fossil record chart used with this paper indicates discovery of birds and mammals in the Jurassic system. Many charts indicate discovery of fossil mammals at a slightly lower level than that of birds. This is predictable since everything points to birds and mammals as having nearly the same RFPP. Then, too, mammals have a generally more massive structure, which would make it more likely for them to survive fossil destruction by weathering.

Conclusions

It is desirable for a hypothesis to lie within the realm of scientific method because then it is possible to put it to a test. The test for this explanation of the fossil record could be an analysis of an extensive, random sampling of fossils from rock strata that formed after the last index fossil, mammals, supposedly evolved.

The rock strata would have to be generally easily accessible and unmetamorphosed. All of the index fossils will be discovered, of course, but I predict that they will be in the same comparative quantity as illustrated in the available fossils triangle. This test would have the effect of verifying the correlation between available fossils and available rocks.

Fossil formation and subsequent discovery, like geology and ecology, are governed by natural laws, therefore, like them it possesses a degree of predictability. I have attempted to explain the predictability of the fossil record in relation to the global flood. In doing so, the hypothesis of evolution in general and two of its basic concepts in particular have been challenged.

Is the fossil record the most direct evidence of evolution as one paleontologist suggests?[33] I contend that the fossil record, in scientific terms, is nothing more or less than a manifestation of available fossils and available rocks.

Does the fossil record support the popular concept that life evolved from the sea? I contend that the presence of marine forms deepest in the series is nothing more or less than a manifestation of pre-Flood habitat (proximity to water).

Endnotes

1. Don L. Leet and Sheldon Judson, *Physical Geology,* third edition (Englewood Cliffs, NJ: Prentice-Hall, 1965), p. 91–92.

2. George Gaylord Simpson, *Life of the Past: An Introduction to Paleontology* (New Haven, CT, and London: Yale University Press, 1953), p. 20.

3. Ibid., p. 20.

4. Ibid., p. 37.

5. G.G. Simpson, Colin S. Pittendrigh, and Lewish H. Tiffany, *Life: An Introduction to Biology* (New York: Harcourt, Brace and World, Inc., 1957), p. 623.

6. Paul A. Zimmerman, editor, *Rock Strata and the Bible Record* (St. Louis, MO, and London: Concordia Publishing House, 1957), p. 128.

7. Cleveland P. Hickman, *Integrated Principles of Zoology,* third edition (St. Louis, MO: C. V. Mosby Co., 1966), p. 536.

8. Ibid., p. 509.

9. Ibid., p. 464.

10. Tracy I. Storer and Robert L. Usinger, *General Zoology*, fourth edition (New York: McGraw-Hill, Inc., 1965), p. 466.

11. Hickman, *Integrated Principles of Zoology*, p. 455.

12. Ibid., p. 436.

13. Ibid., p. 110.

14. Ibid., p. 146.

15. Ibid., p. 158.

16. Storer and Usinger, *General Zoology*, p. 455.

17. Hickman, *Integrated Principles of Zoology*, p. 373.

18. Paul B. Weiz, *The Science of Zoology* (New York: McGraw-Hill Book Co., 1966), p. 621.

19. Ibid., p. 651.

20. Ibid., p. 566.

21. Hickman, *Integrated Principles of Zoology*, p. 110.

22. Norman D. Newell, "Crises in the History of Life," *Scientific American,* 208, no. 2:77 (Feb. 1963).

23. Peter E. Volpe, *Understanding Evolution* (Dubuque, IA: Wm. C. Brown Company, 1967), p. 140.

24. Charles Darwin, *On the Origin of Species* (New York: Random House, Inc., 1859), p. 373.

25. Simpson, Pittendrigh, and Tiffany, *Life: An Introduction to Biology,* p 743.

26. Ibid., p. 25.

27. John J. Fagan, *View of the Earth: An Introduction to Geology* (New York: Holt, Rinehart and Winston, Inc., 1965), p. 161.

28. Ibid., p. 164.

29. Ibid., p. 388.

30. Simpson, Pittendrigh, and Tiffany, *Life: An Introduction to Biology,* p. 37.

31. Zimmerman, *Rock Strata and the Bible Record,* p.130.

32. Ibid., p. 127–128.

33. George G. Simpson, *Horses* (Garden City, NY: Doubleday and Company, Inc., 1961), p. 220.

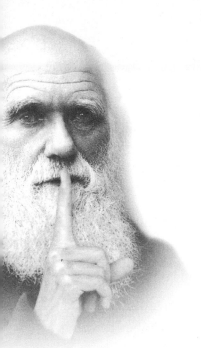

Chapter V

The Episteme
Is the Hypothesis

The real purpose of the evolutionary hypothesis is not the scientific one of explaining the origin of life, for it is impossible to do that, utilizing only natural laws and phenomena. Rather, the hypothesis is dedicated to a philosophical goal: to "ungod the universe." The tool by which that is to be accomplished is what is known as the positive science episteme. This is possible through a widespread and deeply rooted delusion; it is the grand delusion regarding the creation-evolution controversy. It is the popular false belief that evolutionary views are the result of pure, unadulterated, objective science. Nothing could be further from the truth. Alternative points of view about origins such as creation, theistic evolution, and even monstrous births were widely discussed among Charles Darwin's contemporaries.

Today the only point of view given serious consideration in textbooks and most periodicals is atheistic evolution, perpetuating the grand delusion. Atheistic evolution became orthodox, not because it was proved and the other disproved, but because of two opposing epistemes that exist concerning scientific methodology.

An episteme is the "historical *a priori* that in a given period delimits in the totality of experience a field of knowledge. . . ." In other words, a point of view for a particular period of time. An episteme is similar to, but broader than, Thomas S. Kuhn's paradigm, which is "a synthesis of sufficient scientific merit to draw practitioners away from rival theories and which functions as a source of future methods, questions, and problems."[1]

The two epistemes in question are the creation science episteme and the positive science episteme.

The creation science episteme emphasizes mind, purpose, and design in nature, while the positive science episteme holds that scientific knowledge is ". . . the only valid form of knowledge and is limited to the laws of nature and to processes involving 'secondary' or natural causes exclusively."[2] The positive science episteme "avowedly and purposely ungods the universe."[3] Gillespie, in *Charles Darwin and the Problem of Creation,* describes the rivalry between the two sciences as follows:

> Those who argue that there was no real warfare between science and religion in the nineteenth century ignore the presence of these two sciences. The old science was theologically grounded; the new was positive. The old had reached the limits of its development. The new was asking questions that the old could neither frame nor answer. The new had to break with theology, or render it a neutral factor in its understanding of the cosmos, in order to construct a science that could answer questions about nature in methodologically uniform terms. Uniformity of law, of operation, and of method were its watchwords. The old science invoked divine will as an explanation of the unknown; the new postulated yet-to-be-discovered laws. The one inhibited growth because such mysteries were unlikely ever to be clarified; the other held open the hope that they would be.[4]

Unfortunately for the positive science proponents, there are simply too many creationist scientists in the history of science who have made many discoveries and contributions to scientific knowledge to support the assertions in the above paragraph.

Although Gillespie does not point this out, his book confirms what I had previously suspected: the positive science episteme is the hypothesis of evolution. The positive science episteme is simply a polite way of describing a prejudice against any belief in the supernatural. In other words, evolutionary views do not exist to explain the origin of life, rather it exists to make prejudice respectable and acceptable.

Positivists would like to have us believe that the positive science episteme benefits science. The purpose of science, within its limitations, is to investigate and make truth statements about our environment. As to the origin of life, unless someone observes a plant or animal having evolved into another kind of plant or animal, evolution must remain a hypothesis. But by insisting upon excluding special creation or any other alternatives, the positive science evolutionists have destroyed the objectivity and the very purpose of science itself as it relates to the question of the origin of life. Positive science is really a biased policy of exclusion that limits the investigative powers of science and the education curriculum to a belief in evolution.

If, in reality, the episteme is the hypothesis, then that would explain the unscientific techniques that are employed to support evolutionary hypothesis, such as the extravagant use of analogies, which really have little scientific value; the insistence upon having natural selection conceived metaphorically rather than literally (metaphors, of course, are outside the realm of science); extrapolating microevolution as macroevolution; the overriding bias in all of the interpretations of the evidence for the origin of life; and the technique of immunizing evolutionary hypothesis against disproof by mongering in subsidiary hypotheses to explain away and neutralize conflicting facts. Consequently, no matter how many facts contradict evolution, it still must be accepted because the alternative is creation, and creation is contrary to positivism. In other words, evolutionists have the mental capability to be true to positivism, while being unfaithful to science and all the while giving the impression that they are the great defenders and lovers of science. For example, "Joseph LeConte believed in evolution despite what he took to be the adverse verdict of geology because regularly occurring 'secondary causes and processes' were all that science knew, and that meant evolution."[5] LeConte believed in evolution because he believed in positivism, which, of course, begs the question as to how life originated. I would venture to guess that LeConte's attitude is typical of many present-day evolution proponents.

The Bias of the Founders of Evolutionary Hypothesis

There is evidence that the main attraction to evolutionary hypothesis for some of the founders was not the "scientificness" of it, but the negative effect it had on organized religion. Evolutionary views were seen as a way to advance their philosophy while diminishing the influence of religion.

W. R. Thompson states that "the concept of organic evolution is very highly prized by biologists, for many of whom it is the object of genuinely religious devotion, because they regard it as a supreme integrative principle. This probably is the reason why severe methodological criticism employed in other departments of biology has not yet been brought to bear on evolution speculation."[6]

T.H. Huxley may serve as a case in point. Huxley was the self-proclaimed teacher of the hypothesis in England. He took it upon himself to introduce the hypothesis to the public with a series of articles and lectures. Personally, he regarded Darwin's views as merely a "working hypothesis," which is a rather low status; an hypothesis being considered something less than a theory. Yet, he reportedly told his wife, "By next Friday evening, they will all be convinced that they are monkeys."[7] Why the contradiction? Why the desire to convince an awestruck public that the status of the view is anything more than a "working hypothesis"? Perhaps his thinking was influenced by his well-known religious animosity.

John Dewey, one of the founders of the progressive education movement, recognized that "the new logic of Darwin forswears inquiry after absolute origins and absolute finalities in order to explore specific values and the specific conditions that generate it. This has been the most common philosophical import of the *Origin*."[8]

Exclusion of theology and the concept of special creation was looked upon by some as the great virtue of evolutionary views. Julian Huxley, grandson of T.H. Huxley and one of the chief spokesmen for the hypothesis, declared, "He was an atheist, and Darwin's real achievement was to remove the whole idea of God as a creator of organisms from the sphere of rational discussion."[9] In the same vein, Ludwig Plate, a German advocate of the hypothesis, explains that "Darwin's greatest service in his opinion is in the fact that he saw to explain organic finality out of natural forces to the exclusion of any metaphysical principle operating with conscious intelligence."[10]

Ernest Haeckel, another German promoter of the hypothesis, reacted similarly when for him "Christianity had been superseded by a worship of humanity in general combined with enthusiasm for the enlightened minds of classical antiquity and hatred against the ecclesiastical reaction."[11]

Finally, John A. Moore, present-day spokesman for evolution (not to be confused with John N. Moore, a well-known creationist), seems to echo the founders regarding the positive science episteme when, in an article in *The American Biology Teacher*, he laments the statistics that indicate: "Among 16 to 18 year olds, 71 percent believe in ESP, 64 percent in angels, 28 percent in ghosts."[12] He seems to think that it is the responsibility of secondary education to root out belief in the paranormal or supernatural and that the public schools have failed in this responsibility. Moore's regrets are contrary to reality. I do not think a majority of parents are concerned about having their children disbelieve in the supernatural. Nor do a majority of educators think it is their responsibility to indoctrinate students into believing only that which is scientifically explainable. Perhaps evolutionists' concern about the supernatural is that as long as some people believe in it there will also be some who will believe in creation.

I do not mean to imply that everyone who accepts evolutionary views as an explanation for the origin of life shares the same animosity toward theology that Haeckel and Huxley shared, but I do believe that most of them are convinced that the positive science episteme is justified, and consequently their objectivity is jeopardized. The point of all of this is that a scientific hypothesis should stand or fall on its scientific merits and should not be maintained on its philosophical ramifications or a prejudiced episteme.

Sometimes positivism is described under the misnomer of the Doctrine of the Neutrality of Science. Chauncey Wright, an occasional professor of mathematics at Harvard, is credited with this idea. He became interested in evolution shortly after the *Origin* was published to the extent that he carried on a personal correspondence with Darwin and published articles in defense of the hypothesis. Wright's "neutrality" doctrine called upon investigators to be free from the domination of *a priori* systems at all times, keeping ethical sentiments separate from scientific knowledge. Thus, Darwin's system was a scientific hypothesis of biology, a hypothesis that had no necessary causal effect on religious, philosophical, or social matters. Also, evolutionary views were to be presented "with no regard for any considerations that might produce unnecessary and unwarranted 'conflicts' with religion."[13] At first glance, the neutrality concept seems like an acceptable bit of logic until one realizes that if we cannot consider origins theistically, then we must, from lack of choices, consider it only materialistically. The Doctrine of the Neutrality of Science is really a license to consider scientific evidence for the origin of life only from an *a priori* belief in evolution.

Evolution Dogma

Perhaps it would be well to demonstrate how positivism biases the evidence and the curriculum. Let us analyze comparative anatomy, one of the studies that is supposed to supply the hypotheses that make up the hypothesis, and perhaps one of the most impressive when considered exclusively from an evolution bias. Comparative anatomy means to compare body parts, and according to the evolution belief, this means that any time similarities are observed among plants or among animals it is taken to indicate that they had a common evolutionary ancestor. It is quite convincing to see pictures of the skeletal similarities of a turtle and the human being, for example, and interpret the similarities to mean they evolved from a common ancestor. What the student often fails to realize is that one may compare body parts down to the molecular level, but it will never ever tell us how these organisms originated. In other words, comparative anatomy is convincing only so long as the observer *a priori* assumes evolution.

There is no test to prove the evolution interpretation of comparative anatomy. Other nontestable hypotheses in the congeries of hypotheses that make up evolutionary views are geographic distribution, embryology, and vestigial parts. Evolutionists, like pioneer natural philosophers in the past, fail to make a distinction between testable and nontestable hypotheses. Darwin himself, in a letter to Asa Gray, admitted, "I am quite conscious that my speculations run quite beyond the bounds of true science."[14] The history of science reveals a long struggle between those who would neglect and deemphasize experimentation to test hypotheses and those who would give emphasis to it.

Ritterbush, describing 18th century naturalists, reports, "Although the authority of science was invoked on their behalf, the concepts reflected an improper understanding of organic nature, far exceeding the evidence given for them, and too often led naturalists to neglect observation and experiment in favor of abstract conceptions."[15] He also describes them as preferring unlimited explanation based upon speculation rather than limited explanation relying upon experimentation. In a similar vein, Nordenskiold notes, "During the reign of romantic natural philosophy, conditions were different, the representatives of that school, who imagined that they could solve all the riddles of existence by speculation, deeply scorned experiment, which they considered led to fruitless artifice."[16]

On the other hand, Leonardo da Vinci, noted for his scientific as well as artistic accomplishments, insisted upon experimentation: "If experience fails to confirm the hypothesis, it must be abandoned; and apart from positive experimental confirmation it has no value."[17] Rene Descartes, 17th-century science reformer, insisted that hypotheses "must receive a completely cogent demonstration before they can properly be admitted as scientifically valid conclusions."[18] Roger Bacon "saw clearly the value of the experimental method as the only route to certainty."[19] Bacon lived in the 13th century and was a pioneer advocate of experimentation to test hypotheses. (Sometimes critical observation — not speculation — is a sufficient experiment or test.) Advancing to the present time, Dellow states that "experiment is the final arbiter."[20]

Thus we see a unity of thought spanning some 700 years.

Finally, Sir Karl Popper advances the issue further by pointing out the obvious: "A theory which is not refutable by any conceivable event is nonscientific," and "the criterion of the scientific status of a theory is its falsifiability, or refutability, or testability."[21] He also urges investigators to "try again and again to formulate the theories which you are holding and to criticize them. And try to construct alternative theories — alternatives even to those theories which appear to you inescapable; for only in that way will you understand the theories you hold. Whenever a hypothesis appears to you as the only possible one, take that as a sign that you have neither understood the hypothesis nor the problem which it was intended to solve."[22]

We have learned, then, that nontestable hypotheses are not even in the realm of science and that alternative hypotheses should always be considered. Alternatives will introduce skepticism, the forerunner to objectivity. But if nontestable hypotheses are nonscientific, what is their status? What they must be are statements of belief based upon a certain set of facts influenced by the investigator's personal philosophy, religion, or intuition. Others with a different philosophy, religion, or intuition may view the same set of facts entirely differently.

Alternative creation interpretations for the evidence would serve to remove the hypothesis from the realm of scientific dogma. Why not consider creation? The creation reply to the evolution interpretation for comparative anatomy could be: what if similarities are observed? One would expect similarities among organisms under the *a priori* assumption of creation. One would not necessarily expect each kind of organism, all living in the same biosphere, to be unequivocally different in every detail from every other kind of organism. There is no test for either the creation or evolution interpretation for comparative anatomy; consequently, it proves nothing in that it is supportive of both beliefs. Can the creation interpretation be faulted when the evolution interpretation is obviously just as much a matter of personal belief?

Darwin's Confusion

Probably no one was more confused about the question of the origin of life than Charles Darwin. He, of course, rejected the idea of creation and even went so far as to formulate "tests" that, to him, disproved creation. For example, God would only have created distinct species; He would not have made hybridization a possibility.[23] God would not have created rudimentary organs.[24] God would not have created orchids with such an "endless diversity of structure" simply for achieving fertilization.[25] God would have created the blind cave animals of Europe and America, because of their identical conditions to life, to resemble each other closely; instead they are not closely allied.[26] God would not have created plants to be so prodigal in the amount of pollen they produce — only a small amount of which is utilized in fertilization.[27] Well, all that these quaint "tests" tell us, of course, is how Darwin would or would not have created. Apparently the positive science episteme does, after all, allow consideration of creation, but only if it is considered in a negative context.

Darwin also rejected theistic or designed evolution, the idea held by some of his contemporaries that the evolutionary process was somehow under the direction of God. His reason for rejecting theistic evolution was that it "was but a disguised form of special creation."

> I entirely reject, as in my judgment quite unnecessary, any subsequent addition "of new powers and attributes and forces"; or of any "principles of improvement," except insofar as every character which is naturally selected or preserved is in some way an advantage or improvement, otherwise it would not have been selected. If I were convinced that I required such additions to the hypothesis of natural selection, I would reject it as rubbish. . . . I would give nothing for the theory of natural selection if it requires miraculous additions at any one stage of descent.[28]

Theistic evolution had to be rejected by Darwin because it ran contrary to the positive science episteme in that it failed to "ungod the universe." Also, it made his mechanism for evolution, natural selection, superfluous. If variations and/or selection was preordained, there was no point in even considering the mechanism. Evolution simply became a slowed-down version of creation.

Rejection of special creation and theistic evolution leads us to the one remaining option — chance or atheistic evolution, which is taught in the typical textbook. One would think that this must be where Darwin stood. But, no, we find that he also rejected chance. In a letter to Asa Gray he wrote:

> I grieve to say that I cannot honestly go as far as you do about Design. I am conscious that I am in an utterly hopeless muddle. I cannot think that the world as we see it is the result of chance; and yet I cannot look at each separate thing as the result of Design.[29]

Late in his life, in a conversation with the Duke of Argyll, the duke commented to Darwin, "It was impossible to look at the numerous purposeful contrivances in nature and not see that intelligence was their cause." Darwin "looked at [him] very hard and said, 'Well, that often comes over me with overwhelming force; but at other times,' and he shook his head vaguely, adding, 'it seems to go away.' "[30]

Having rejected creation, theistic or designed evolution, and atheistic or chance evolution, Darwin seemed to have been in a hopeless muddle on the question of the origin of life. Gillespie concluded that he died with some vague notion of theism. It seems reasonable that, if Darwin's hypothesis is taught, his confusion on the subject should also be part of the curriculum.

Present-Day Attitudes

The Victorian generation has long since passed away and this generation has become the jaded inheritor of a scientific revolution, some aspects of which inspire fear and dread rather than the old confidence. Science and technology are now viewed through the baleful eyes of those who have discovered their "hidden worms," mainly in the form of environmental degradation and health hazards. The new public attitude toward science and technology is plainly noted in a recent issue of *Science*:

> Important to the future of science and technology is the fact that the public has somewhat lost confidence in the ultimate value of the scientific endeavor. It is not that they hold pure science or scientists in any less esteem. But they are less certain that scientific research will inevitably yield public benefit.
>
> For the first time in centuries, there are thoughtful persons who are not morally certain that even our greatest achievements do, indeed, constitute progress. To some philosophers it is no longer clear that objective knowledge is an unquestioned good.[31]

In a *Time* magazine essay entitled "Science: No Longer a Sacred Cow," the author called the moon explorations the grand finale in the continued rise of the prestige of science. Contrast excerpts from the *Time* essay with Macaulay's description of science and technology cited earlier:

> Sure enough, down it [prestige] went. And in its place has risen a new public attitude that seems the antithesis of the former awe. That awe has given way to a new skepticism; the adulation, to heckling. To the bewilderment of much of the scientific community, its past triumphs have been downgraded, and popular excitements over new achievements like snapshots from Mars seem to wane with the closing words of the evening news. Sci-Tech's promises for the future, far from being welcomed as

harbingers of Utopia, now seem too often to be threats. Fears that genetic tinkering might produce a doomsday bug, for example, bother many Americans, along with dread that the SST's sonic booms may add horrid racket to the hazards (auto fumes, fluorocarbons, strontium 90) that already burden the air.

The new skepticism can be seen, as well as heard, in the emergence of a fresh willingness to challenge the custodians of our technical knowledge on their own ground. It is most conspicuously embodied in the environmental crusade and the consumers' rebellion, but is also at play across a far wider field. It applies to public light and political heat to Detroit's automotive engineers, who for generations had dispatched their products to an acquiescent public. It encompasses protests against the location of dams massively certified by science, to open disputes about the real values of scientifically approved medicines, and the increasing willingness of patients to sue physicians to make them account for mistakes in treatment. Sci-Tech, in a sense, has been demoted from a demigodhood. The public today rallies, in its untidy way, around the notion that Hans J. Morgenthau put into words in *Science: Servant or Master?*: "The scientists' monopoly of the answers to the questions of the future is a myth." The fading of this mythology is the result of Americans' gradual realization that science and technology's dreamy wonders sometimes turn out to be nightmarish blunders. Detergents that make dishes clean may kill rivers. Dyes that prettify the food may cause cancer. Pills that make sex safe may dangerously complicate health. DDT, cyclamates, thalidomide, and estrogen are but a few of the mixed blessings that, altogether, have taught the layman a singular lesson: The promising truths of science and technology often come with hidden worms.[32]

The Role of Education

The time has come to dispel the grand delusion and reject the positive science episteme. It is time for education to establish its own criteria upon the evolution curriculum. Darwin as scientist does not qualify as Darwin as teacher. The criteria that Darwin used to develop his hypothesis are not up to par as the criteria used to teach the hypothesis. In other words, positivism in education means indoctrination.

Following are some of the curriculum objectives that I have developed over a period of ten years. They serve to remove evolutionary views from the realm of scientific dogma so that one may teach rather than indoctrinate. To begin with, the congeries of hypotheses that one finds in the typical textbook, and most of which Darwin used in the *Origin*, should be categorized into testable or nontestable hypotheses. The basic hypotheses would then be categorized as shown in Table 1.

An educator need not teach any particular account of creation, which would probably require the teaching of all accounts of creation. Creation should be considered only in relation to the scientific evidence presented for evolution, without any theological elaborations. When this is done, it becomes obvious to students that the textbooks are biased and that the nontestable hypotheses may be interpreted satisfactorily for creation. A creation consideration of the nontestable hypotheses immediately removes the hypothesis from the realm of scientific dogma. It is, of course, contrary to the positive episteme because it no longer ungods the universe, but education must reject positivism.

Concerning the testable hypotheses, one must consider the unthinkable — does evolutionary hypothesis pass or fail tests? In most cases, the test is simply a critical observation of our environment. For example, Darwin never observed natural selection and was forced to use imaginary examples in the *Origin*. If natural selection is not observed, why isn't it?

To ask whether or not evolutionary views pass tests is based upon the following alternative: To use the vernacular, the bottom line in evolutionary hypothesis is that chance can create an intelligent design; this

Table 1. Testable and Nontestable Hypotheses Contrasted

TESTABLE HYPOTHESES	NONTESTABLE HYPOTHESES
natural selection	comparative anatomy
artificial selection	geographic distribution
mutations	embryology
fossil record	vestigial organs

is what is taught in the typical textbooks. The alternative is that our ability to reason as human beings is the result of creation rather than chance. Remember, also, that science is basically a reasoning process. If that is true, it would mean, then, that any scientific hypothesis that denies the existence of God would have to be unreasonable, unscientific, and in some way or ways subject to disproof. The creation alternative requires that we ask ultimate questions — evolution or dogma does not.

Conclusion

The point that I wish to make is that a distinction is made between testable and nontestable hypotheses, which allows for consideration of creation. My personal experience of including a creation alternative indicates that parents have rejected positivism and its biased policy of exclusion. Educators must be prepared to do likewise. The old convoluted logic of positivism that evolution must be accepted because it is forbidden to consider alternatives has no place in education. For those who are philosophically committed to evolutionary views, the problem is obvious — they must decide whether or not they can place professional standards above personal beliefs.

Endnotes

1. N.C. Gillespie, *Charles Darwin and the Problem of Creation* (Chicago, IL: University of Chicago Press, 1979), p. 2. In Greek, *episteme* means "understanding." Aristotle sometimes used it for science *par excellence.*

2. Ibid., p. 3.

3. Ibid., p.15.

4. Ibid., p. 53.

5. Ibid., p. 151.

6. W.R. Thompson, *Science and Common Sense* (London, New York: Longmans, Green, 1937), p. 229.

7. L. Huxley, editor, *The Life and Letters of Thomas Henry Huxley*, Vol. 1 (New York: D. Appleton and Co., 1902), p. 205.

8. J. Dewey, *The Influence of Darwin on Philosophy* (New York: Peter Smith Co., 1951), p. 13.

9. N. Macbeth, *Darwin Retried* (Boston, MA: Gambit Inc., 1971), p. 126.

10. E. Nordenskiold, *The History of Biology* (New York: Tudor Publishing Co., 1928), p. 572.

11. Ibid., p. 506.

12. J.S. Moore, "Dealing with Controversy: A Challenge to the Universities," *The American Biology Teacher* 41(9):544-547 (1979).

13. P. Weiner, *Evolution and the Founders of Pragmatism* (New York: Peter Smith Co., 1969), p. 78.

14. N.C. Gillespie, *Charles Darwin and the Problem of Creation*, p. 63.

15. P.C. Ritterbush, *Overtures of Biology: The Speculations of Eighteenth-Century Naturalists* (New Haven, CT: Yale University Press, 1964), p.1 and 156.

16. Nordenskiold, *The History of Biology*, p.370.

17. E.H. Madden, editor, *Theories of Scientific Method: The Renaissance through the Nineteenth Century* (Seattle, WA: University of Washington Press, 1960), p. 15.

18. Ibid., p. 49.

19. G. Schwartz and P. Bishop, *The Origins of Science* (New York: Basic Books, Inc., 1958), p. 36–37.

20. E.L. Dellow, *Methods of Science* (New York: Universe Books, Inc., 1970), p. 24.

21. K.R. Popper, *Conjectures and Refutations* (New York: Basic Books, Inc., 1962), p. 36–37.

22. K.R. Popper, *Objective Knowledge: An Evolutionary Approach* (Oxford: Clarendon Press, 1972), p. 265.

23. Gillespie, *Charles Darwin and the Problem of Creation*, p. 72.

24. Ibid., p. 68.

25. Ibid., p. 77.

26. Ibid., p. 77.

27. Ibid., p. 126.

28. Ibid., p. 120.

29. Ibid., p. 87.

30. Ibid., p. 87.

31. P. Handler, "Public Doubts about Science," *Science*. 208(4448):1093 (1980).

32. F. Trippett, "Science: No Longer a Sacred Cow," *Time*. 109(10):72–73 (1977).

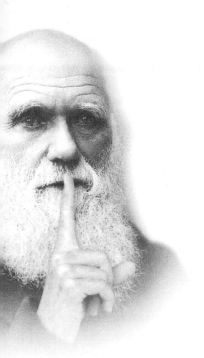

The Principle of Applied Creation in an Origins Curriculum

Introduction

The evolution-creation controversy has become increasingly intense over the last decade, and the public education system seems to be caught in the middle. Creation proponents are insisting that their point of view also be taught in what is usually described as the two-model approach. Evolution proponents, on the other hand, for various reasons are insisting that creation continue to be excluded from the curriculum. The arguments for and against a two-model approach are well documented. As educators, we should consider ourselves sovereign on the issue and, doing our best to be neutral, resolve it in a fair and equitable way.

What I am advocating and what I have taught for many years is something less than the two-model approach involving an extensive curriculum in scientific creationism. The problem for education is the brazen bias in the present evolutionary curriculum; consequently, the creationism that I have been using in the curriculum has the specific purpose of eliminating bias. This is called applied creation. It is scientific creationism only to the extent that it eliminates bias. It stands to reason that if an evolutionary interpretation or hypothesis for some evidence concerning origins cannot be proved, then one is really only expressing a personal opinion; the creation point of view for that particular evidence should also be considered. I am not advocating scientific creationism; I am advocating honesty and objectivity in the curriculum. I know of no other way to eliminate bias than to consider creation, the other obvious alternative.

The Curriculum Strategy

Since 1969 I have taught a curriculum on origins that includes creation and, after several years of classroom experimentation as to how creation should be incorporated, settled upon the curriculum strategy described here. The following curriculum description is based upon Darwinian evolution, but it is a strategy that has universal application for all scientific theories of origins. In the curriculum, the concept of creation is general, meaning life coming into existence fully developed by miraculous power. A detailed description of creation, such as the Judeo-Christian account, could create problems with students of other beliefs. The concept of creation becomes legitimate, in fact necessary, if evolutionary theory is taught as follows. First, rather than thinking of evolution, per se, one should consider it as a collection of hypotheses or evidence interpreted to substantiate the general hypothesis. Next, one should categorize the main hypotheses on the basis of whether they are testable or nontestable. A typical textbook will reveal that comparative anatomy, geographic distribution, comparative embryology, and vestigial parts are the basis for nontestable hypotheses. What is the status of a nontestable hypothesis? According to Sir Karl Popper, a noted authority on scientific methodology, "A theory which is not refutable by any conceivable event is nonscientific. Irrefutability is not a virtue but a vice."[1] In reality, a nontestable theory or hypothesis is a statement of belief based upon a certain set of facts influenced by the investigator's personal philosophy, religion, or intuition. It is not in the realm of science.

Analyzing the Hypotheses

With the foregoing information in mind, a teacher may present students with alternative hypotheses representing both the evolution and creation influences upon the investigator. Both the creation and the evolution interpretations that follow could be elaborated on, but that would not change the fact of their nontestability.

Geographic Distribution

Geographic distribution refers to the way plants and animals are distributed on earth. For example, if we see one kind of turtle on one island and a different kind on another island not too far away, or if we find kangaroos in Australia and nowhere else, the evolution hypothesis holds that plants and animals are in their present location because that is where conditions were right for them to evolve. Of course, there is no conceivable test to prove this hypothesis, which is why students should be allowed to consider the creation hypothesis.

The creation hypothesis suggests the following. Plants and animals were specially created and were at one time widely distributed on earth, but many kinds have become extinct except in isolated places. There is no test to prove this hypothesis either, but students should not be denied consideration of it.

Similarly, we do not know if the several species of finches presently found on the Galapagos Islands are the result of evolution from an original species or the remnant populations of species once widespread on earth.

The reader will note that the concept of creation serves the utilitarian purpose of eliminating bias from evolutionary hypotheses that are not in the realm of science anyway.

Comparative Anatomy

Comparative anatomy, which means to compare body parts, is probably the most impressive evidence that a student will encounter, when considered exclusively from an evolution point of view. According to the evolution hypothesis, this means that any time similarities of structure are observed among plants or among animals, it is taken to mean that they had a common evolutionary ancestor. It is quite convincing to see pictures of the skeletal similarities of a turtle and a human being, for example, and interpret the similarities to mean they evolved from a common ancestor. What the student often fails to realize is that one may compare body parts down to the molecular level, but it will never ever tell us how these organisms originated. In other words, comparative anatomy is convincing evidence only so long as the observer *a priori* assumes evolution. There is no test to prove the evolution interpretation for comparative anatomy; one would have had to be there to observe the transformation.

The creation hypothesis for comparative anatomy could be: what if similarities are observed? One would expect similarity among organisms under the *a priori* assumption of creation. One certainly would not expect each kind of organism, all living in the same biosphere, to be unequivocally different in every detail from every other kind of organism. There is no test for either the creation or evolution interpretation for comparative anatomy; consequently, it proves nothing in that it is supportive of both *a priori* assumptions.

Comparative Embryology

The catch phase "ontogeny recapitulates phylogeny" is often heard in reference to embryology. This means that the development of the embryo reveals an evolutionary development. It is often pointed out that the human embryo at one stage has folds in the neck region that bear a superficial resemblance to gills. Nevertheless, these folds develop into tubes, glands, and other neck parts. G.H. Waddington wrote, "The type of analogical thinking which leads to the theory that development is based on the recapitulation of ancestral stages or the like no longer seems at all convincing or even very interesting to biologists."[2]

Other authors also express a similar opinion of the value of embryology as evidence for evolution. Yet in the textbooks, one often sees a series of pictures comparing the embryos of man, fish, chicken, and so on. A youthful high school student certainly lacks the knowledge and maturity to make a judgment on the quality of this evidence. From the creation point of view, if one expects similarities among the adult forms, one would also expect to see it in the embryonic forms, not only because they all exist in the same biosphere, but because most embryos originate similarly as a single fertilized egg. There is, of course, no test to prove either the creation or evolution hypothesis for embryology.

Vestigial Organs

The term "vestigial organs" refers to organs of structures in plants and animals that have no use or for which no use has been discovered. In other words, these are organs that allegedly are left over from evolution or are in the process of evolving into something useful. The trend, though, has been to discover uses for organs and structures once thought to be vestigial. The human endocrine glands were once thought vestigial, as was the coccyx, or the so-called tailbone. The coccyx has muscles attached to it and is necessary for proper movement. No definite use has been discovered for the human appendix, although some authors report that it may function as a defense against some diseases during infancy. Fifty or 60 years ago, for investigators to say an organ was vestigial was just another way of admitting their ignorance as to its purpose.

In order to expand one's thinking on a subject, it is sometimes useful to consider the source. Let us analyze Darwin's thinking on this evidence as presented in *On the Origin of Species*. He uses the word *rudimentary* to mean an organ or structure that has lost its function, and *nascent* to mean "a part that is capable of further development." The wing of the penguin gives us an idea of the extremely speculative, nontestable quality of this evidence. Darwin raises the question as to how we can know if a part is rudimentary or nascent: "The wing of the penguin is of high service, acting as a fin; it may, therefore, represent the nascent state of the wing; not that I believe this to be the case; it is more probably a reduced organ, modified for a new function."[3]

This is an interesting statement. He begins by admitting that the wing of a penguin functions as a fin, which is to say that it is neither rudimentary nor nascent. He then goes on to speculate that the wing may be in a nascent condition — in other words, to eventually be used for flight — but then adds that it is more likely in a rudimentary condition, having lost its use for flight.

All of this, of course, is pure speculation based upon his belief that life evolved to the exclusion of creation. Why not consider creation? Why not consider the possibility that penguins are flightless birds specially created to exist in their present niche in the ecosystem? Why must everyone think that penguins have a need for flight or had a need to give it up?

He also points out in this chapter that "in the mammalia . . . the males possess rudimentary mammae."[4] If male mammary glands are rudimentary, then at one time they had the ability to secrete milk. On the other hand, the male mammary glands may be in a nascent condition, which would mean that males may someday have the incongruous ability to feed but not bear offspring. Or perhaps males will also develop the ability to bear offspring, thus eliminating the role of opposite sexes. Obviously, this is all nontestable speculation, so why exclude from consideration the possibility that males were created with rudimentary mammary glands? The concept of creation does not require every organ to have a function, have had a function, or eventually acquire a function. Evolution theorists cannot prove that what appears to be a rudimentary part ever had a use, and often what appears to be rudimentary is later discovered to be useful.

We are obligated to teach the hypothesis this way because, much as one may wish it were not so, depending upon his or her bias, creation has not been disproved nor evolutionary hypothesis proved. Scientifically speaking, absolute proof of evolution would be the documented, eye-witnessed report of plants or animals having evolved into other kinds of plants or animals. But because of the infinite lengths of time associated with evolution, a phenomenon of this kind is not likely to be witnessed by human eyes.

Incorporating creation into the nontestable evidence for evolution, rather than teaching creation and evolution separately, overcomes some very serious problems. For one thing, creation is not actually being taught; it is simply acknowledged as a viable alternative and serves as a curriculum tool to remove evolution from the realm of scientific dogma. When it comes right down to it, excluding the creation alternative forces one to concede to a modern fallacy, namely, that fellow human beings — scientists with no greater intelligence, insight, or overall ability than anyone else — are omnipotent, all-knowing, and superhumanly unbiased on the all-important question of the origin of life. I don't think we should make that vital concession. A scientist who is making an investigation into an on-going phenomenon such as photosynthesis may be relied upon to be completely objective, but when it comes to the question of the origin of life, with all of its philosophical ramifications, I prefer to consider alternative interpretations for the evidence and I think students should do likewise.

Creation serves the important purpose of revealing to students the unscientific plasticity of the evidence. It reveals, for example, how Darwin could look at penguin wings as being either rudimentary or nascent. Since this speculation is not scientific anyway because it is not falsifiable, one might just as well speculate that penguins were created with wings just the way they are. One of the objectives of applied creation is to determine whether any evidence is compatible to evolution and not creation. What evidence is actually testable and substantiates evolutionary hypothesis while excluding creation? Or what evidence is actually testable and refutes evolutionary hypothesis?

The Fossil Record

For the sake of brevity, let us review one type of testable evidence, the fossil record that has been given considerable attention throughout the book. The fossil record has recently been acknowledged as the vital failure of Darwinian evolution by some evolutionists.[5] We have previously discussed other testable evidence such as the failure to observe evolutionary natural selection and the observation of limited rather than unlimited variability. The problem of the fossil record is, of course, the absence of intermediate fossils (fossils that are not quite reptiles, fishes, mammals, etc.), large numbers of which the hypothesis predicts should be found. Lest anyone should think that the lack of intermediate fossils is a conclusion to be credited to the objectivity of present-day researchers, I wish to remind the reader that this fatal contradiction was known and reported by Georges Cuvier, the father of paleontology, before *On the Origin of Species* was written. Coleman describes Cuvier's opinion of the fossil record as follows:

> He based his entire refutation upon the incompleteness of the fossil record. If the fossils could not show us the course of the supposed transmutations, what reason was there to believe that these unusual events had actually occurred? The fossils were our only record of life in the remote past, and their lesson was obvious and not at all, Cuvier believed, what the transformists would have liked it to be. Not a continuous series of almost similar creatures but rather an interrupted sequence of dissimilar forms was what was discovered.[6]

A notable comtemporary of Darwin's, Asa Gray, father of American botany, reached a similar conclusion.

> Why, it is asked, do we not find in the earth's crust any traces of transitional forms? The lame answer is that "extinction and natural selection go hand in hand." In other words, traces of the higher forms exist, but the transitional ones, having served their ends, are lost![7]

Himmelfarb reports that T.H. Huxley, "Darwin's bulldog," was compelled to agree with Gray and Cuvier about the fossil record.

What does an impartial survey of the positively ascertained truths of paleontology testify in relation to the common doctrine of progressive modification? It negates these doctrines, for it either shows us no evidence of such modification, or demonstrates such modification as has occurred to have been very slight, and, as to the nature of that modification, it yields no evidence whatsoever that the earlier members of any long-continued group were more generalized in structure than the later ones.[8]

What we can conclude from the absence of intermediate fossils is that it is reliable evidence that contradicts Darwinian evolution, but does not contradict creation. We must not conclude any more than that for creation nor any less for evolution.

At least those are the results when the scientific method is rigorously applied. Jevons, in *The Principles of Science: A Treatise on Logic and the Scientific Method*, states, "A single absolute conflict between fact and hypothesis is fatal to the hypothesis."[9] The rule is easy to state but difficult to apply. Rigorously applied, Darwin should not have written *On the Origin of Species*, being well aware of the absence of intermediate fossils.

The rule of conflicting facts is often rendered ineffective by an unscientific process that is not pointed out often enough to students learning scientific methodology. The unscientific process to which I refer is known as hypothesis-mongering. Basically what happens is a subsidiary hypothesis is introduced to explain away the conflicting fact, thus preserving and protecting the primary hypothesis, rather than allowing it to fall.

Subsidiary hypotheses have validity only if they have some basis in fact; if not, science quickly degenerates, at least for the particular question being addressed, into the chaos of personal opinions. It requires an almost superhuman effort to accept a conflicting fact for a pet hypothesis and refrain from hypothesis-mongering. The rule of conflicting facts serves to preserve the integrity of science, while revealing its limitations in making truth statements about our environment.

Another aspect of the fossil record that we should consider is the basic premise in evolutionary hypothesis that a fossil can be assumed to be an evolutionary ancestor to organisms living today. This assumption is based upon an *a priori* belief in evolution. There is no way to prove that a fossil is the evolutionary ancestor to anything living today. From a creation point of view, a fossil may really be an extinct species having no evolutionary relationship to anything. To illustrate the point, the picture of fossils of alleged horse evolution — which were in only three out of seven recently published textbooks that I checked — could be legitimately criticized. Namely, the fossils were found in several states throughout the Midwest and not in consecutively deeper rock strata. The fossils may represent animals that were contemporaneous, some of which have become extinct. To illustrate the point further, one could lay out partial remains of a pig, antelope, white-tailed deer, elk, or moose, for example, and say that they represent the evolutionary ancestry of the moose.

The same conditions apply to fossils evidence of alleged human evolution. The very primitive specimens may simply be extinct animal primates, while the more human-appearing fossils may actually be extinct human races, none of which have any evolutionary relationship to human beings living today.

There is only one event that could dispel the obvious conclusion that intermediate organisms never existed, and that is to discover the large numbers of intermediate fossils that evolutionary hypothesis predicts — a number large enough to make it unquestionable; a few questionable fossils will not do the job.

It is often brought up by students that the average height of Americans has increased over the years and that this is evidence for evolution. If that were the case, then we would have to say that the reason for this phenomenon is that short people are consistently choosing to marry much taller people or that short people are not surviving and therefore not producing as many offspring. Blinded by evolutionary dogma, we fail to consider alternatives, one of which might be that we have simply become products of a technological environment. Internal combustion engines and electric motors have virtually eliminated all manual labor for everyone, as well as walking. Child labor has long been outlawed in industry, and the few remaining family farms have been mechanized. We have become a sedentary population compared to what we were not too many years ago.

Along with this condition we have more food available than ever before, including fresh meat daily, thanks to refrigeration. Couple a more or less sedentary existence to an abundant food supply and we may have the answer to an increasing height and more obesity. It is the same principle that farmers use when growing animals. I think it is safe to assume that a more active lifestyle with less food would result in an overall decrease in size.

I would ask the reader to review a typical high school textbook and compare its treatment of evolutionary hypothesis to what is actually known about the views in the upper echelons of science. Are the gaps in the fossil record mentioned? Probably not. It is rare that a paleontologist will mention gaps in the fossil record in professional journals. Occasionally this does happen.

Despite the bright promise that paleontology provides a means of "seeing" evolution, it has presented some nasty difficulties for evolutionists, the most notorious of which is the presence of "gaps" in the fossil record. Evolution requires intermediate forms between species and paleontology does not provide them.[10]

Check the textbooks again. Are there any statements at all that question the reliability of any of the evidences for evolution or imply its theoretical rather than its factual nature? Compare your estimate of the textbook treatment of evolutionary hypothesis with the following quotes.

In accepting evolution as fact, how many biologists pause to reflect that science is built upon theories that have been proved by experiment to be correct, or remember that the theory of animal evolution has never been thus proved?[11]

. . . the macromolecule-to-cell transition is a jump of fantastic dimensions, which lies beyond the range of testable hypothesis. In this area all is conjecture. The available facts do not provide a basis for postulating that cells arose on this planet.[12]

Finally, we must ask ourselves whether or not evolution proponents, who more or less determine the textbooks' treatment of evolutionary hypothesis, are guilty of a vast deception regarding its true status.

Conclusion

Some people may object that this curriculum strategy "picks on" evolution, but theories exist to be criticized. We have discussed how applied creation relates to Darwinian evolution, the hypothesis presently in vogue among most evolutionists, but applied creation has universal application to all scientific theories of origins past, present, or future. The use of applied creation centers on what is not testable about them, allowing creation to come into play, thus preserving objectivity.

We should be receptive to our students. In the absence of absolute proof of evolution, we know that creation must exist in the minds of many of them. Should we not be willing to consider the evidence from their point of view also? I suppose it is none of our concern should evolution theorists consider the evidence for the origin of life exclusively from an evolutionary point of view, but it is, as the saying goes, a horse of a different color to expect an educator to do likewise. It is irrelevant for an educator to claim a kind of scientific immunity, as some evolutionists do, and protest that creation is not within the realm of science — not when the natural explanation for the origin of life has not been proved nor the supernatural explanation disproved. What if the supernatural explanation were true?

We educators should not go along with the evolution theorists whose excuse for excluding an alternative for consideration is based upon some kind of scientific *modus operandi*. We must appeal to a higher order of things — call it "freedom of thought." We must not allow the bias in evolutionary hypothesis to manifest itself in a biased curriculum. Let evolutionists interpret the evidence to exclude creation; we must interpret the evidence to include both evolution and creation. While formulating a hypothesis, a theorist remains in the realm of science, but when it comes time to teach a hypothesis and it involves public education, then it must be done according to the standards of education.

If the investigation of origins is done out of genuine scientific curiosity, the purpose of which is to attempt to make truth statements, within its limitations, about our environment, there should be no objection to contrasting the evidence to the concept of creation. On the other hand, if the purpose of investigating origins is the philosophical one of discovering a way to "ungod the universe," then that motivation would reveal itself in an unwillingness to consider the creation alternative. Applied creation serves the utilitarian purpose of eliminating biased interpretations of the scientific evidence for origins. It seems to me that we must accept a small measure of creation in the curriculum or endure a large measure of bias.

Because applied creation is a curriculum tool tied to Darwinian evolution, it would self-destruct without it. But because it is also an educational principle based upon an educator's obligation not to deny students access to varying points of view, it would rise again, phoenixlike, whenever unscientific speculations or nontestable hypotheses about origins are incorporated into textbooks or educational films, consequently insuring objectivity in the future.

Endnotes

1. K. Popper, *Conjecture and Refutations* (NewYork: Basic Books, 1962), p. 36.

2. G. Waddington, *Principles of Embryology* (London: George Allen and Unwin, 1956), p. 10.

3. C. Darwin, *On the Origin of Species* (New York: Random House, Inc., 1972), p. 346.

4. Ibid.

5. "Man, a Subtle Accident?" *Newsweek* (Nov. 3, 1980): p. 95–96.

6. W. Coleman, *Georges Cuvier, Zoologist: A Study in the History of Evolution Theory* (Cambridge, MA: Harvard University Press, 1964), p. 338.

7. A. Gray, "The Origin of Species," *The North British Review*, 32:456 (1860).

8. G. Himmelfarb, *Darwin and the Darwinian Revolution* (London: Chatto and Windus, 1959), p. 272.

9. W. Jevons, *The Principles of Science: A Treatise on Logic and the Scientific Method* (New York: Dover Publications, 1958), p. 516.

10. D. Kitts, "Paleontology and Evolutionary Theory," *Evolution*, 28:467 (1974).

11. C. Darwin, *The Origin of Species* (London: J.M. Dent, 1971), introduction by L. Matthews.

12. D. Green and R. Goldberger, *Molecular Insights into the Living Process* (New York: Academic Press, 1967), p. 407.

Join the
Conversation

Ask the experts

Build relationships

Share your thoughts

Download free resources

Creation
Conversations
.com

This is your invitation to our
online community of believers.